ONE, PLEASE!

THOMAS H. JOHN

Ordering Information:

Prime Seven Media
518 Landmann St.
Tomah City, WI 54660

Printed in the United States of America

A Welsh Boy's memory of events during the 1960s '70s and '80s; progression through schooling, University and life thereafter.

TABLE OF CONTENTS

GLOSSARY 1

PROLOGUE 3

MY EARLY LIFE, ... 5

VERY EARLY MEMORIES OF MY LIFE IN A WORKING CLASS ENVIRONMENT 7

MY PARENTS AND MY JUNIOR (or 'Primary') SCHOOLING 8

MY FATHER 10

MY JUNIOR or, 'Primary' SCHOOLING. 13

My junior school sports memories 16

MY SECONDARY (or 'Comprehensive school') SCHOOLING 17

YEAR BY YEAR CHRONOLOGY. 25

THE END OF MY SECONDARY SCHOOLING. 58

LIFE AS AN UNDERGRADUATE. (1979 -82) 68

PRE - REG. PHARMACIST TIMES 75

LIFE IN EAST LONDON. 78

MY DALLIANCE AS A CHEMIST SHOP'S PROPRIETOR. (1986- 88) 82

SOUTH WOODFORD 83

TAWE PHARMACY 88

MY YEAR LONG SOJOURN TO THE BAR VOCATIONAL COURSE, AND MY SUBSEQUENT YEARS IN LEGAL PRACTICE. 90

PUPILLAGE ODDYSEYS. 104

TROUBLE AT HOME? 109

LIFE AFTER MARRIAGE: MIDDLE AGED PURSUITS 112

ACKNOWLEDGMENTS 116

LEISURE ACTIVITIES AND MY MUSICAL TASTES AND ADVENTURES IN PARTICULAR. 117

POSTSCRIPT. 119

GLOSSARY

BVC = Bar Vocational Course.

Dining = The programme of (in those days, 18) 'dinners' one had to attend as a BVC student before being entitled to be called to the bar. Nowadays, I believe the qualifying number has been reduced to 9.

GCE = General Certificate of Education.

Megaloblastic anaemia American – Anemia) = Condition where individual blood cells are pathologically enlarged due to disease.

MV = Motor Vessel.

Ph = Pharmacopeia.

WFH = Work(ing) from Home.

PROLOGUE

The purpose of this book is to describe past days in the life of an individual living in one of the most civilised countries on Earth.

The 'modus operandi' of this book will be to describe the every day experiences of a person (me) that some might describe as being on the autistic spectrum, the so-called Autistic Spectrum Disorder; or 'ASD'

Can one be on the Autistic spectrum, albeit, in no way 'Disordered'?

There is a recognised medical condition called Autism Spectrum Disorder (ASD). I have occasionally complained of being on this spectrum. But I have never been medically diagnosed as a sufferer.

By this book's conclusion, I hope that if you yourself believe that you are such a person, that is to say, one who is in the Autism spectrum, you will find the knowledge and experiences herein helpful and useful in your daily life.

If you are NOT such a person yourself, but you know, meet with, socialise with or even give periodical care, to such a person, you too will gain valuable, and informative insight into their psyche.

In short, you may be able to better understand them.

MY EARLY LIFE,

pparently, I was born during the early morning of Sunday, December 11th 1960.

I write 'Apparently' as of course, I have absolutely no personal recollection of the event itself!

Both my parents have now been dead for several years. My only sibling, my sister, was not yet born. But, there is still in existence, one, single item of tangible proof of my birth's occurrence namely; a Bronze coloured, metallic 'Christening Cup'.

Christening Cups were mementos in which it was fashionable to give to the Christian parents of a new born baby in my part of the UK during, the 1950s and 1960s and likely, the years pre-dating my birth too. I write this because, on family visits, my cousins, aunts, uncles and my own grandparents all had their own 'christening cups' on display in their houses' display cabinets. Usually, they were in a prominent location, and their purpose seemed to me to be very much in order to 'Show-off' the family's new arrival to visitors!

My entire family was, very much, a type of aspirational working-class. My 'Christening cup' is actually dated the 8th January 1961. This was the date that the christening ceremony occurred in my local Christian chapel on the first open date it had available after my birth and NOT on my actual date of birth!

I am reliably told that the birth occurred at Neath general hospital, a National Health Service (NHS) facility in South Wales at that time, It served the towns of Neath, Briton Ferry, and Port Talbot and their surrounding areas and villages such as Margam, Taibach, Aberavon and Cwmafan. (Cwmavon).

At that time, the NHS would only have been in existence for just over a decade, and was an emanation of the socialist government that had achieved a remarkable landslide victory in the general parliamentary election of 1946, the first such election following the cessation of the hostilities of the Second World War (1939-1945), The NHS has now of course, grown to almost monolithic status and proportions.

I am not sure it would have made any difference to the rather reserved, and dowdy, fashions of that post - war period whether it was the conservatives that had been victorious at the 1946 general election or not. After all, the Conservative Party had been the party in government from as far back as 1951 and until the mid 1960s so the election of socialists to office may have been viewed as little more than an electoral aberration. The Labour Party itself had only came into political prominence in the early 1920s and came from a political movement that sought to give the ordinary, working, man a 'voice' in the form of a vote for the politician of his free, democratic, choice.

No doubt, academic opinions may vary on this, but certainly, my extensive family were all working class and I believe that the overwhelming majority of them would have voted for the socialist political candidates of the political parties of the time.

Britain was, in either event, having to recover from 6 years of privation after the end of the WW2, which had ended on 6th June 1945.

VERY EARLY MEMORIES OF MY LIFE IN A WORKING CLASS ENVIRONMENT

At the time of my birth, the Prime Minister (Harold Wilson)'s era of the 'white heat of technology' was still the best part of a decade away, wartime food rationing was still in place, the house where I was to be raised was still without mains electricity or electric light, so gas street lighting was still in use outdoors, and there was only candlelight available indoors in some of the less developed local villages and areas. In fact, I well remember visiting some of my family's relations who lived in a neighbouring town, being visited by a 'Lamp Lighter' every evening at sundown - when an elderly - looking (to my young eyes) man who mounted the street's lamp standards every evening at dusk, so that residents could benefit from street lighting as they came to, and from, their places of daily work. Usually, those people would have been travelling on foot, the lamplighter would have to climb up his heavy, wooden portable ladder while holding his glowing lamp mantle, and touch the hot mantle on to the piped source of natural Gas, the toxic gas carried through gas mains pipes in most places, so that it caught light and bestowed what seemed to be a very dim intensity (by modern day standards) of incandescence , initially being red in colour, then changing to orangey colour and finally, yellow light to the street below after what seemed a long time!. It was not until around a decade later that Sodium electric lighting became commonplace in my part of the world. That would have been the first time that white street lighting was seen by the majority of the population.

MY PARENTS AND MY JUNIOR (or 'Primary') SCHOOLING

My father, William Emlyn John and my mother, Thelma Mary (also John but not, of course, blood-related although bearing identical surnames- names)), had, I was told first met each other at a Port Talbot Hospital social event sometime in around 1958. My mother was nursing at the Port Talbot General hospital, in Hospital Road, which was situated a few hundred yards from the bech, its 'Promenade' and, soon, the new Afan Lido sports centre and where Aberafan (or Aberavon) becomes the 'Sandfields' housing estate. This is NOT the same site as is used for the current Neath Port Talbot hospital. Before my birth, my mother actually survived the 'Asian' 'flu epidemic of 1958 (my mother claimed she had spent weeks in an isolation ward at the hospital having gone down with the condition whist at work nursing others!).

Had she not survived of course, I would never have been around to write this memoir!

Neither of them was particularly young at the time. My Father had been born in Abbey Road, Port Talbot on 30th August 1920. My mother was born in a house in Mount Street, Morriston (a suburb of Swansea) as the younger of 2 identical twin sisters on 6th December 1925.

The 2 locations are around 10 miles apart so, would have been relatively inaccessible to each other at that time. But I believe that one of the factors linking them was that both were members of the Welsh language speaking community. This factor could well have served as a sort of social glue. An important factor the pair had in common.

My (by now) now late mother, who, at that time, was employed as a state registered nurse (SRN) worked for the local NHS Health Authority and, in the post WW2 socialist infrastructure was admitted to a bed on the 'Maternity' wing as the era's attitude to medical indications and, no doubt, recommendations for a mother's first-born child (a Prima gravide) tended to preclude home births. The usual practice was to hospitalise for the birth and then embark on a nursery period of up to 10 days post - partum!. That type of 'pidgin' Latin was a device used, and gloried in, by the educated medical professionals of the time, that is to say, the Doctors and nurses of the time. I am unsure whether this fashion for the use of quasi - grammatical Latin extended to other professionals also linked to the practice of medicine (eg physiotherapists, pharmacists, podiatrists, chiropodists, hospital porters) and the like. But, I recall my late mother's habitual use of medicalised language giving the impression that she and her colleagues were bestowing their skills and knowledge to their patients, all of whom were deemed by them to be on a lower hierarchical rung than she, and the rest of the medical professionals would have been.

None of this is in any way intended to disparage my memories of my mother.

But I still recall aspects and elements of an 'age of deference' to still be operative at the time.

My mother had done her initial nurse's training at the old Swansea Hospital which was situated at the junction of Swansea's main thoroughfare of the Queensway, and Saint Helen's Road. She had first become a student nurse at the height of World War II (in 1943) and remembered first hand, the 'Swansea Blitz' of that year when the German Luftwaffe, over several nights attempted to raze the town of Swansea, including its sea port to the ground.

MY FATHER

*A*s already set out, my father was born at one his Aunts house, in Abbey Road, Port Talbot, with his parents (my paternal grandparents: Thomas Jenkin John and Mary-Ann Evans). Abbey Road Itself still stands and is almost exactly on the boundary of the main-line railway lines and several sidings tracks adjacent to the Margam steelworks. The Luftwaffe were targeting this region of Wales during the 1943 blitz- principally owing to the nearby dockyards in Swansea and neighbouring Port Talbot, both because of their carrying of maritime cargoes to and from Swansea docks and the presence of the steel plant in Margam (a region of Port Talbot) that originally dates back to medieval times).

With only one exception, (due to having contracted Tuberculosis in the late 1930s and being confined to 'Craig Y Nos' hospital near Brecon), my father never left Port Talbot; save for the fortnight;s annual holidays taken from work. He died aged 82 in spring 2003, at Neath-Port Talbot general hospital having not only survived, but recovered from his Tubercular infections. I remember him being advised to attend medical X - ray appointments every so- often to check he had not relapsed or if the TB flared up. It never did. He was finally given a completely clear bill of health sometime around the late 1970s.

Having the ability to manufacture steel for the war effort, the Margam plant was able to produce both steel in ingot form and in sheets of steel. The nation's Railways could therefore be constructed and maintained, and all manner of motor vehicles assembled likewise. This was especially useful to the British war effort not to mention after the war, during the period Britain was recovering from, and rebuilding, after WW2 and this role continued through the 1950s, '60s, '70s and early '80S.

Overall therefore, my early life was founded on a firm bedrock of economic stability if not outright prosperity.

Both my parents were capable of work and did so without interruption - save that my late mother made the choice to pause her career while both me and my younger sister were infants and toddlers and until we had both started our mainstream schooling.

My father had worked throughout; from the outbreak of war in 1939, until his forced redundancy in 1982 when cuts to the workforce were enforced by the then managers of the Margam steel plant under the aegis of the plant's chairman, Sir Monty Finniston, a political appointee..

From Autumn term 1967 until both parents ceased work, therefore, our family was a 2 - income family.

We could therefore afford annual summer holiday breaks where we would stay in (always British!) seaside resorts for at least a fortnight each time.

The first family holiday I remember was spent at a hotel in Ilfracombe, Devon. Ilfracombe was a favourite holiday destination for my father. Although the round trip from Port Talbot to and from by road is, according to AA or RAC sources, a 180 odd mile trip in one direction, there is a more direct way - via sea travel!

In those days, an organisation known as 'The White Funnel Fleet' ran pleasure boat trips on the Bristol Channel, (a body of sea between the North Devon and South Welsh coastlines). The trips were run on on a frequent basis over the summer seasons and ran to and from Swansea harbour, and Mumbles and Porthcawl piers and from Penarth near Cardiff. They also ran from Bristol harbour itself and used various ports and harbours in North Devon such as Lynton, Lynmouth and Ilfracombe itself. Any putative passenger would consult the relevant timetable for a convenient sailing, pay the fare and board. Advance booking was possible, but rarely necessary. Return trips from north Devon sailed from Ilfracombe, Lynton or Lynmouth. Another popular calling point for these services from all those destinations was Lundy Island, itself situated in the middle of the Bristol Channel and surrounded on all sides by the sea. We, as a family, went on that trip at least once. I remember that, there being no pier on Lundy, the boat would have to drop anchor near enough to the Island for a rowing boat to collect Lundy-bound passengers and, arrangements could then be made for return journeys from Lundy to the Fleet boat; and then back to Swansea, or wherever convenient on the South Wales side. Almost invariably, this would have to be the venue we started from. Typical journey times were 2 hours in one direction, so, after an early start, we could spend several hours ashore and still be back in Swansea between around 8, 9, or even 10pm. After factoring in the several hours at our North Devon destination, we could have several hours on shore to spend as we wished - a visit to restaurant or kiosk selling Fish & Chips, pubs for those old enough. Plenty of walking venues around town, or even a dip in the sea itself providing you had remembered to pack your bathing trunks and a dry towel at the start of the day.

Sadly, those days are now just historic memories for us, and we were among the lucky children of the 1960s.

The names of the steamers that served on general public duty for the White Funnel fleet were the 'Cardiff Queen', the 'Bristol Queen', the 'St Trillo', and the 'Balmoral'. There is now a just solitary member of The White Funnel Fleet in public service. This is 'The MV Waverley' which divides it's public journey times between the (very) occasional Bristol Channel trip and its (more frequent) trips on the River Clyde in western Scotland.

MY JUNIOR or,
'Primary' SCHOOLING.

My first ever experience of formal, state administered schooling, came in around the year 1964, or 1965.

The school was called 'Groes' school one was situated in the eponymous village. The village has now ceased to exist and, in reality, lies somewhere beneath the Eastbound carriageway of the M4 motorway between Junctions 38 and 39!

I spent only the 1 term there, which must have been autumn terse.

I was quite shy in my demeanour, the more so because, in contrast with my 'Nursery' school, which was run in and by, my father's non - conformist chapel, I didn't really know any of the other children or any of the teachers.

I DO remember that, unlike my home, or my father's family and associates, nobody ever spoke in the Welsh language at Groes school. That contrasted with speech at my bi-lingual home.

I have a memory of the class' teacher. She seemed to be quite elderly, thin, grey or white hair, and rather impatient. The only lesson content I can still remember is when she declared to us pupils, that 'I' and 'S' is 'IS'. She then repeated that phrase numerous times in a rather tired sounding monotone!

Some of the other pupils seemed either, to have difficulty in either remembering that concept, or perhaps, they just didn't appreciate it's importance as a grammatical device.

I'm pleased and rather relieved to be able recall that, straightaway, I understood the concept perfectly well!

I wonder how many of my contemporaries have any recollection of that occasion. After all, it is now over 60 years ago!

Whatever may have been the merits, or de merits, of Groes primary school, it ceased to exist sometime in 1975 after the last compulsory purchase order for the land at Groes was executed. Groes primary School, a few houses and the famous 'Round Chapel' of Margam were destroyed, or re-located, to nearby locations. The round chapel itself was fully reconstructed, and now stands about a mile away from its original site in Tollgate Road, Margam. It is still in use, and has a small, faithful congregation.

My parents (both native Welsh speakers) must have taken the decision to have me moved to a 'Welsh' school In reality, a bi-lingual, English and Welsh languages tuition establishment.

Thus, I was enrolled as a pupil at 'Pontrhydyfen' Welsh primary school. There, I spent the next 6 or so years until outgrowing my primary education years in 1972.

The school itself was finally closed only as recently in 2009 and its shared school yard is now the site of a privately occupied house. The house, and former school, stand on a hummock in the lower Afan Valley at the elevation of the 'Oakwood' hamlet within a couple of hundred metres of a now disused aqueduct which, over a century earlier, had fed local metal working plants and foundries with water for their smelting, and other, operations.

It is still eminently possible to reach these locations, which form such a memorable part of my childhood from by use of either the A4107 trunk road, or the adjacent B4286 road between Port Talbot and Cymmer Afan.

From the latter Road, the hummock is accessible via a set of concrete paving steps up from river level. There are 2 sections to the step way, which are set at right angles to each other. A recurring memory of my having to use those steps on a daily basis is of such trivia as having to trudge UP the steps at the beginning of each school day in all weathers whereas, of course, one could bowed DOWN the same steps whenever school was out at the end of each day!

Now, that I am halfway in to my 7th Decade, the steps seem pretty steep. Still, climbing them keeps one physically fit!

Finally in relation to my earliest years, straddling my first, and second decades, I remember being absolutely transfixed by the TV coverage of the USA's 'Apollo' space programme and its moon missions. I clearly remember the triumphant manned missions, from Apollo 8 over Christmas 1968 to the programme's final abandonment after the Apollo 17 mission in December 1972. I lapped up every nugget of information I could lay my hands on at the time. Unfortunately, I was fast asleep when the first live pictures from the moon surface were transmitted in the early hours of Monday

20th July 1969 (Well. I WAS due at School the following day)! Apparently, my father managed to stay awake, and I confess, I was rather jealous of him as he relayed his verbal account of the night's drama over our family breakfast the next day. Apollo 12 then followed to the moon's surface in November 1969. Of those readers who can recall or are interested in memories of those times, who, of those who saw it, can ever forget the pure drama of the Apollo 13 mission in the spring of 1970? There occurred an explosion on board the moon bound spacecraft resulting in the crew's having to return to earth without visiting the moon's surface. The lives of the crew were in mortal danger over the 3 or so days it took the spacecraft to turn around, get back to Earth AND splashdown safely.

My last term in junior school was in the spring of 1972. I found it a wrench leaving. Some of my schoolmates were set to go to the same secondary school as I was going and so, we managed to stay in touch with each other afterwards and when each of us embarked on our careers and life's work., But one or two went on to other secondary schools or education providers and so, there are a handful of erstwhile schoolfriends that I have now completely lost touch with.

I still recall our school's (probably 'Un-official') 'Leaving Party' that we pupils were given at the end of the summer 1972 term. It was held under a red brick, former railway viaduct in a field below the school building in Pontrhydyfen. A faint historical memory of that time arose from the time when Miss Samuel, my form teacher, announced one morning after assembly, that each of us pupils should listen out for the sound of a train passing along the viaduct. The sounds of passing trains had been a constant, albeit, rather unobtrusive, feature of my schooldays up to that point in time. I remember listening - I think it was around the middle part of the school's day, and hearing the train chugging past. After it had gone, she dramatically announced that none of us would never, ever, be able to hear that noise again. The line was to be closed! I have checked the historical record which records that the line actually closed on 10th November 1964! But, from my memory alone, I would swear that it must have been a few years later that all rail traffic finally ceased. There is a commemorative plaque on the approach to a platform near to the village of Cynonville which is only a few hundred yards along the same stretch of line, records that section of line not closing until 1970. That seems to me to be much nearer the mark. After all, I would not have been physically able to recall an event which occurred before I had ever set foot in any place within earshot! Equally, I would have been far more able to record and recall events that occurred when I was around 10 years of age, than I would when aged only 4 or 5. My account that you are now reading must, therefore be the accurate one!

My junior school sports memories.

As our school's yard was a concrete section of ground, We would have to play any our school's soccer and baseball fixtures and games on grass. We had to climb down to the grass field down a steep bank while, at the same time, being careful to avoid the Cow - pats, stinging insects, stinging nettles and whatever other natural hazards that were, or may, have been present. Thorns from Gorse bushes growing on the bank were particularly painful!

All the school's competitive games, as well as many of our practices occurred at a field called 'Rhyslyn' (pronounced 'Rusling)'. This was accessed my walking the 200 or so yards in our stockinged feet from our school's gate to the nearby stone Aqueduct which crossed the river Afan. Then, we would turn to our right at right angle, past a few stone cottages until we got to a point high above the Rhyslyn field (normally, the venue for Pontrhydyfen's senior rugby team). And then, we would have to literally 'slide' down to the pitch level by sliding down a steep, wild bank, and being careful not to get stung by the gorse bushes and stinging nettles along the way. The only concession that I can recall being granted to the 10 and 11 year olds as older boys, was that we had permission to change into our studded football boots BEFORE leaving the school's gates. Only then could we walk as far as the stone aqueduct, turn past the cottages and proceed to the playing field itself. The 'Click/Clacking of our studded feet must have been audible to all those living nearby as we 'marched' (always 2 abreast) to play our football games.

MY SECONDARY
(or 'Comprehensive school')
SCHOOLING.

My last year in junior (known colloquially as 'Ysgol Gynradd') or, in English; 'Primary' School, aka 'Junior' School therefore came to an end with the long school summer holiday in 1972.

That particular 6 week break was dominated by the need to be fitted out with my new 'school uniform'. This comprised clothes incorporating my new school's 'colours' - a black wool Blazer adorned with the school's badge, it's motto incorporated in to its desig; the school's necktie, in the school's blue and green striped colours, and either white shirts or, at least, shirts coloured in the school's approved colours of light grey or light blue.

It was only after actually starting school during the 1st week in September of 1972, that us new boys discovered that we had been rather fortunate in terms of our school uniforms! I have yet to meet any of the girls from my class, or year, who actually confessed to liking her school uniform of a blue and green striped pinafore dress OR a light green top with an azure, light, dark or navy - blue skirt. Apparently, the school, which dated only from 1969 (and had formerly been a boy's grammar school) so I was part of only its third annual intake of pupils. It's infrastructure including it's buildings, classrooms, offices and even it's kitchens had been appropriated by, and due, to the then socialist national government's plan to end all appearance of favouritism on grounds of personal wealth or social status. Even the name of the school was designated 'Comprehensive' rather than the then established grammar or secondary modern schools. Instead, new pupils were merely placed within grammar or secondary modern stream, that is to say, those pupils expected to perform well academically and within the upper quartile would be placed in the grammar 'stream' and assigned to relevant classrooms accordingly. These children would have the opportunity to study those subjects such classical Latin (although for some reason- not Greek!), some modern languages such as French and German, the classical sciences, music and drama. By contrast, those children assigned to the secondary modern stream were taught such subjects as woodwork and metalwork The secondary modern stream girls were given tuition in cookery and needlework. Accordingly, the comprehensive school system had difficulty accommodating any academiclly inclined boy who wanted to study cookery or any academically inclined girl who preferred metalwork to needlecraft! I remember special dispensation having to be given to pupils who, for whatever motive or reason, wished to study a subject set in conflict with their gender at birth.

My time at this comprehensive school lasted until the break up of the spring term in 1979. By then, all final exam papers had been taken although, no one anticipated that the results would be published before August.

For any former pupil with my academic capabilities, this meant progression to university. I recall that the favoured academic/vocational courses among most of my erstwhile classmates were Medicine, Dentistry or Chemical Engineering (Chem. Eng.)!

Candidates would either have to apply directly to the institution(s) they were interested in, or take their chances with a central agency known as 'UCCA' (the Universities Central Council for Admissions).

This institution would liaise with up to 5 different university colleges to attract the suitable students to their offered courses.

Typically, one would apply to the university college of interest well in advance of the 'A' level exam result date simply in order to achieve the tactical advantages of having had an introduction to the institution concerned. Ideally, one would be invited for an informal interview with the institution's admissions tutors pending publication of the candidate's actual 'A' level grades.

Those who failed to achieve the desired, or anticipated grades would be faced with a choice of beginning work at a non-academic organisation such as a High Street Bank, a factory or an apprenticeship to a trade or calling. Alternatively; if still intent on attending a university, they would enter a 'clearing' process whereby universities who, for whatever reason, had failed to attract sufficient interest from potential undergraduates could sill admit the student to their academic course.

Buoyed by pure enthusiasm, I suspect rather than realism, I had initially applied to 5 different medical schools as my choices.

Unfortunately, none were interested in me, either as one of my initial 5 choices or in the subsequent 'Clearing' process for unsuccessful candidates..

Equally naturally, and easily understandable, I was very disappointed.

But, fortunately, work colleagues of my mother's suggested that I try applying to a University college that offered ranges of subjects allied to medicine.

I still am unaware of the exact mechanism, but one day I received a package in the Royal Mail post from The School of Pharmacy, University of London. It contained a brochure for the school, a prospectus AND, a written invitation to attend an interview at the school.

An interview date and time were duly arranged and, at the appropriate date and time in the summer of 1979, I found myself on a London bound train, fully suited and booted and anticipating what would prove to be the day my life was transformed.

When I arrived at the school's address at 29-39, Brunswick Square, Bloomsbury, London WC2, I noticed that the building seemed to be so quiet. I reminded myself that many of the staff would still be on summer leave and walked up the smallish terrace of steps to be able to open the school's entry door. I recall that the actual reception desk was directly opposite the entrance door, around 25 yards across a marbled section floor.

I crossed the floor and saw that there was a quite severe looking, middle-aged woman sitting at the desk. 'Ja'! she boomed in a thick, Germanic contralto voice which might have done justice to Sieglinde, Elda, or some such Wagnerian operatic character. A voice which, I suspected might have knocked many people backwards! 'Oh Hello' I practically whispered back. 'I'm here for an interview'. Djust vait zere!' came the reply. She picked up her telephone and rang someone after first drawing shut, a glass screen between me and she.

Within seconds, a much more attractive and much younger woman appeared and smiled at me. I remember that she had dark coloured dyed hair in a short, and contemporary late 1970s style. It turned out that it would be she that would be accompanying me to the Dean's office. 'But, don't worry, it's on the ground floor, so we won't have to use the lifts or climb any stairs'

I gingerly followed the young woman around a corner where, after a few more paces we came to a rather grand looking, tall, wooden door with 'Dr F. Fish: Dean' inscribed on it in gold coloured lettering.

The young woman knocked the door and it was answered by an older looking woman. After a brief pause, 'Come in' said the older woman. She turned out to be the college/school's Dean's secretary and we had many conversations regarding various things and aspects of the school's work over the next 3 years.

The young woman left. I never saw her again! I guess she may have been just a 'Temp', hired by the school to cover permanent staff's absence, perhaps on holiday or, god forbid, sickness leave.

The older woman I soon discovered, WAS 'permanent staff. She was The Dean's personal secretary.

'I'll take you in now' she said.

I nervously and, I suppose an independent on - looker might have described my outward appearance as 'gingerly' - entered the Dean's office.

I don't recall whether any gesture such as a handshake was offered by either of us; but I do remember seeing a slight, silver haired, bespectacled man of late, middle age and wearing a lightish coloured suit, looking across at me.

'So! You want to read Pharmacy, do you? he enquired.

Oh. Yes! I replied.

This short exchange puzzled me a little. Why else did he think I was there?

'Tell me what you think a pharmacist does' he said.

I don't know what answer the Dean had expected to get. I suspected he would get a 'works in a chemists' type riposte from the majority of the interviewees from my station of life, But even I had learned through having observed the world I had grown up in, listened to my parents over the years, and having a sudden surge of adrenaline, or inspiration, or both, I sensed I was being given an opportunity:-

'Oh, well he makes up people's prescriptions' I ventured.

'Yes. And is there anything else you know about pharmacists'? he went on.

At that point I recalled not only my numerous visits to the local 'Chemist's' shop in Port Talbot over the years - by then, almost 19 years - the smiling faces of the shop staff, the chemist him or herself, his, or her 'nostrums'; the brightly coloured large carboys adorning the upper shelves, the 'Chemist' or "Chemists themselves, always, seemingly adorned in a white lab. coat, the presence of other people of all ages, but especially, those people's prosaic acute states of health, some of them breathing heavily, noisily, wheezingly, some shivering, almost all coughing, using their personal tones of un - wellness, their individual styles and voices - deep coughs, spluttering coughs, weak, feeble coughs, some people expectorating goodness knows what diseased humours into their handkerchieves and most of them would actually be LOOKING ill. The babies and children among them crying, some more noisily than others ; their mothers mainly, and, sometimes vainly, attempting to comfort them.

But of course, I also recalled that my own mother would be encountering the hospital's own pharmacy staff during her daily nursing duties.

'Oh, I suppose you could work in a chemist shop or a hospital's pharmacy department'.

Anywhere else? he asked.

'Ummm'……..

'What about the pharmaceutical industry?' he suggested.

'Yes, I had forgotten about them! Oh……, and, and the people that work here!. Teaching other people about pharmacy'

This, I still believe, was the short, verbal exchange that secured my place to study at the school. Perhaps I was demonstrating something of an open mind; that I was not intent on shutting my mind to the existence of my possibilities for a future career in an occupation closely related to medicine. One that I would need an academic degree to be able to enter.

'Well' said The Dean……….'.I am pleased to be able to offer you a place at the school'.

I immediately felt relieved, satisfied to the point of elation and already formulating what I would say to my parents about the interview's outcome.

Would I try to find a working telephone kiosk nearby in order to break the good news?

If there WAS one near the school and which was also in an un - vandalised state of repair, did I have enough 5, 10, 20 or 50p pieces to successfully make the call in those now far - off, pre - smartphone times?

Due principally to my rather reserved psyche, but also, to varying degrees;[the fact that any nearby public telephones might be out of working order or there being far too many people in front of me in the queue], I decided to head straight back to Paddington train station to get the first train back home. Yes, it would be well over 4 hours before I finally opened our family's front door, but, of course, my good news would still be the same……..!

By the time, I got back to my parents' house, it was mid evening, so both parents were home. Naturally, both were delighted at my news!

We sat and talked.

It was obvious that the rest of that summer, right the way to term's start date on 4th October 1979 would be dominated by the need to equip myself with a new, and complete, set of clothes including an autumn/winter supply, casual clothes, sports outfits and perhaps, something more formal!

The academic terms were each 10 weeks long, so, even the 1st term would not be over until mid December.

I must remember to pack sufficient casual clothes and sportswear. After all, had I not played rugby at school? Had I not just completed the local newspaper 'The Western Mail's own sponsored Marathon race over the summer in a time of 4 hours 11 minutes?. Had I not been a school 'prefect' in my final year in mainstream education? Oh, I felt like quite the young man about town!

I honestly think that the news that I would have to leave home in Port Talbot pleased my younger sister more than anyone else!

There had been signs of filial strain between us for a while. Perhaps since she attained the age of puberty. In fact, I remember my mother taking me to 1 side when I was around 11 or 12 years old myself, to tell me that it was likely that she would 'change' soon, without really advising me of any change's implications.

I now remember the (then recent) occasion which occurred sometime in 1978 when, as we were both about to embark on our make, or break, years at school, in my case to begin my GCE 'A' levels and in her case her 'O' levels, we both got off the school bus completely laden with new textbooks. She also happened to be struggling to carry the final practical cookery exercises of her own academic year's endeavours. I had, I suppose, rather selfishly asked her for some help, as we were both struggling to complete the 100 or so yards to the front door. Of course, there being no mobile, or smart- phones in those days, one would only have been able to either summon help from an independent passer by or neighbour, or break up the short distance by stopping to rest.

Neither of us were prepared to do that!

Neither of us were prepared to sacrifice a few moments of humility toward the other.

But her reaction appeared to me, at least, entirely disproportionate to what was at stake.

She exploded with rage!

'Wot the 'ell? Can't 'ew see I've got my 'ands full too'?

I have to concede my own selfishness at this point.

Trying to weigh either sibling's degree of difficulty or relative plight would be futile in the heat of that moment.

The proper course would have been for either one of us to give way. It would have cost the 'loser' no more than a few moments, and, perhaps, in my case, the risk to the physical integrity of a state owned textbook. But that was not the way our late teenaged minds worked.

To this day, I cannot recall if, or how, the dilemma was resolved. But the episode had somehow left a bitter taste!

In the event, it would not be a long time before my sister and me were to part company for years. She to work in the telecommunications field and me for a separate and entirely un connected existence.

We, as a pair, had precious little by way of common, interests, we had different social connections, even different political viewpoints and different musical tastes.

The verbal explosion between our different, competing personalities, would not come to a head for nearly 5 decades. In fact, it wasn't until over 40 years later, in the wake of the death of our mother, at the age of 96, that the final, verbal showdown happened. It happened at our erstwhile family home in Margam. It happened during broad daylight hours and just a day or so after my mother's funeral service.

I still cannot see what possible motive there was for my sister's verbal outburst at that time or in that specific place! But, it was not pleasant. I walked out of the house. I was determined that I wouldn't go back to the house ever again. The house that both me and my sister had been brought up in. The house that had held so many memories. The house where all our family's triumphs, disasters, controversies, near misses and victories had occurred. The house where, in fact, my dear paternal grandfather had spent his final hours, had died in November 1966, the bed and bedroom he had been confined to, where he, and I had had our last ever conversation, me, standing at the foot of his sick bed, he, in bed but talking to me about the imminent Guy, Fawkes night. I recall him asking me whether there would be 'Jackie Jumpers'? These 'Jackie Jumpers' were a colloquial term for a type of firework, one that exploded when lit, but also then jumped off the ground for a short distance making it a suitable object for inclusion in firework collections used domestically and, along with Catherine Wheels, sky rockets and the like, made up domestic assortments of fireworks. I even remember the name of the firm that produced these firework collections - 'Brock's' Fireworks.

So, although November 5th 1966 would only have been the 5th firework night since my birth, and probably been only the 2nd or 3rd I could possibly have been aware of or remember, this annual institution was already sufficiently familiar to me to have been able to remember such things as the sense of anticipation that I and all the other boys in my class at junior school would have as the 'big night' approached, and then, the feelings of anti-climax on November 6th when the only tangible evidence of our firework displays were the remains of spent firework shells littering our streets, gardens and nearby roads.

The only other memory I have of 1966 was of my class at junior school's appearance in the National Eisteddfod.

For any readers unfamiliar with this event, it is an annual gathering incorporating all types of performance arts, artists and attended by the general public upon payment of an entrance fee.

The Eisteddfod has no fixed venue, but its location alternates yearly. In even numbered years, it is held in South Wales. In odd numbered years it will be held at a venue in North Wales. For those venues in central wales (venues such as Presteigne, Welshpool, Newtown, Aberystwyth and the like, decisions as to venue are made somewhat arbitrarily.

1966 happened to be Margam's year! The Eisteddfod has not been held anywhere in the Port Talbot area since; let alone been back to Margam since. It's baby sibling, the 'Urdd' Eisteddfod did, in fact come to Margam in 2025! It is extremely unlikely to return there in my remaining lifetime.

I remember some, although by no means all, of the salient arrangements for our school's appearance; it had been decided that we would perform a non - competitive dance in a 'Tableau' setting. We were to be dressed in Chinese style tunics, rice picker's wide - brimmed, flat hats and we would be partnered with one partner of the opposite sex. My partner was around a year (or maybe, even 2 years) older than me but, in any case, from a family known to my own parents.

I could still name her. Accordingly, much of the time at spent school during the preparation was spent getting the details right.

The actual day of my appearance on the stage at the 1966 eisteddfod was a grey, sodden occasion with dark, low skies, rain, cold and a very muddy field to dance on!

YEAR BY YEAR CHRONOLOGY.

There now follows, in detail, but purely from my un aided memories, a year by year account of my reminiscences from my idyllic childhood:-

1963 - 67

1963 is the 1st year that I remember any real detail from. The one, specific, detail is of an iron, or steel tricycle that must have been given to me on my 3rd birthday or as a Christmas present from my parents, or possibly grandparents or close relatives. (the 2 dates are in any case, exactly a fortnight apart). It was brightly painted, in darkn blue, but it had solid iron wheels that were coloured red on a white background. I retained it until I received my 1st ever pushbike when I was around 10 years old. I had wanted a bike for at least 2 or 3 years prior to the latter's materialisation but, for some reason, my parents did not procure one. Maybe, this was because we lived on a busy-ish side road with the main A48 trunk road very nearby. I have no doubt that they always would act in my (and my little sister's) best interests. So the only harm that would ever have ensued would have been that I was the youngest, or almost the youngest, boy in my street to get a bike! It would NOT have been the sad fate of those few, fortunately rare children who were killed in road accidents. One of these children was a little girl who belonged to one of my mother's extended family. She was killed before I was even born so, I could. never have known her personally. But my mother always claimed she had been knocked over when running across a road to buy an afternoon ice cream after school one day. She had lost her life. Accordingly, both me and my sister were told never to mention her in the presence of her own parents. Her parents were distant relatives of ours. That my well explain my mother's reluctance to allow us to ride bikes along our street.

1965

The autumn term, which ran from around September to Christmas of 1965, marked the first time I would have been eligible to attend mainstream schooling. Prior to this, I spent some time in a 'Nursery' School. This was run, probably voluntarily, by some of the ladies from my parent's chapel and so I recognised the (exclusively female) 'Teachers' through their attendance at the same Welsh, independent chapel that my parents attended. Everything and everyone was a familiar, friendly face, and I felt very safe there.

But in autumn 1965, I became of the age where schooling was compulsory.

I recall being sent to a village school (sadly, which Is no longer in existence- with more on the reason, later!). It was situated in a tiny hamlet called 'Groes'. I only spent 1 term there. There were no familiar faces and I did not much like it very much.

Although I remember very little beyond what might, with hind-sight, have been my 1st classroom-bound lesson, one occurrence still stands out!. Firstly, the class' teacher, in particular, appeared to my young eyes like what an old woman and should look like. Much older than my mother or my aunties although, possibly, a similar age to my erstwhile nursery schoolteachers (and indeed, seemingly, the majority of the women who attended my parents' chapel).

This woman repeated and kept repeating a single phrase. 'AI AND S IS IS': 'AI AND S IS IS': I AND S IS IS' ad nauseam. I don't recall her saying anything else during the entire lesson. She would repeat this phrase with such fortitude that she MUST have meant it. Her degree of fortitude I found strangely attractive and I certainly have never forgotten this lesson nor it's mode of delivery. I found it very monotonous. I had got the message pretty much immediately she had finished the first 'Ai and S is IS' and, in doing so, ! I had learnt my first formal word. At least, it had taught me the correct spelling for the nominative case of the verb 'To Be'

Her punchy rendition of the word was, I suspect, aimed principally at the less intellectually able boys and girls who were present in that class.

My paternal grandparents lived in a neighbouring street to ours in Margam. Like our house, it was a 3 -up, 2 - down semi - detached house built during the late 1920s or early 1930s. It had a long 'back' garden, where my grandfather grew and tended, an Apple tree; Rhubarb plants, and an array of ornamental flowers and shrubs but had only a few square yards of 'front' garden. Although each end of the semi detached road was accessible to car traffic, it was too small for anything bigger than an SUV. in reality, most people driving their cars into, or out of, the road would use one of the 3 or 4 little side roads along its length for both access or egress.

During this period, my maiden Aunt, Elaine, also lived in my grandparent's house. My aunt Elaine was my father's sister. She was 11 years younger than he was. I liked my Aunt Elaine. She was 'cool', she liked socialising and frequently seemed to be getting ready to go out to a dance or some social event with her best friend, whom I knew as, and called, my 'aunty' Dorothy. Dorothy lived in a neighbouring town called Briton Ferry, was engaged to be married and always seemed to be in a good mood.. I'm not sure how she and my Aunt Elaine first met, but at this time, both had been employed at the large, local steel plant at one time.. The two 'hit it off' together and seemed, to me, to be inseparable thereafter.

My specific memories of my father's own mother are very few. She had been quite frail in the lead - up to her death. In fact, she died of Pernicious Anaemia on 8th May 1965. 'Pernicious anaemia' is a so called' Megaloblastic' condition due to a nutrient (Folate) deficiency, which results in the the shape of the red blood cells in a sufferer's circulation being adversely affected). She was aged 72 at the time of her death. As events transpired, it was some time before its true cause was. revealed. I feel that, in those days, people did not tend to seek 'answers' from doctors or public authorities for something which inevitable awaits us all. My only actual memory of her is of being at my grandparents' house in Beechwood Road, Margam, awaiting my grandfather's return from his sojourn, (which would have been his habitual afternoon stroll with some of his friends), and the presence in the house of my father's only sister - my Aunt Elaine, as one evening meal time approached. My grandmother was crouched over the stove, with her back to me, manipulating some sort of foodstuff which was sizzling in a frying pan. These days, with medical practice, knowledge, and corresponding treatments on offer whether mental and/or, physical, my late grandmother would likely have lived several more years than she actually did, as nowadays, pernicious anaemia is readily, and completely treatable by having daily Cyancobalamin (vitamin B12) supplements by mouth or, less often, by depot injection. The medical biology's mechanism was known, even back then: Pernicious anaemia is a 'megaloblastic' anaemia affecting the shape, (or 'morphology') of certain of the body's blood cells. The missing factor is produced in the body's digestive tract. It is deficiency of THIS, which means the body cannot absorb the vitamin from our diet alone.

At some point during this time, I recall sitting in our family's lounge in Wern Road. It must have been during the evening, because my father was present. As family members we always tended to occupy the same chairs - these were free standing, but thir positions never varied in all the years my family were in occupation; my father on a long reclining sofa facing the TV screen over his right shoulder. The TV itself occupied the square room's opposite corner. I would occupy the area of floor opposite the TV screen and finally my sister, when she was old enough, tended to sit near my father and would have normally viewed the screen over the direction of her right shoulder.

The TV set itself, in common with most of my classmate's sets was a rental model. Every so often, my father would go to the hirer's place of business in the town: a shop called 'Rediffusion' and pay the rental sum due for the period. Nowadays, I guess people tend to own their TV sets outright, with or without there being any rental to pay for its day to day use!

That form of 'Hire - Purchase' arrangement had become very common in the early and mid 1960s. Although It was not until 1974, that parliament enacted the 'Consumer Credit Act' 1974 (c39) and its nowadays 2006 update in conjunction with some of the relevant provisions of 'The Enterprise Act 2002'. The mass production of privately owned motor cars and their easy availability had been fuelled by the boom in consumer credit facilities from the 1960s.

This was just one of the principal means whereby consumers could 'acquire' property, goods or services in those days. Days where the memories and practices arising from the second World War were still relatively fresh in people's minds and, I suppose, affected their daily habits

My Aunt Elaine (1931 - 2017) worked in the general office of the steel plant in Port Talbot during most of the 1960s and, in common with very many of her work colleagues, she was basically an Anglophone. Any smattering of conversational Welsh speaking that she had was restricted to what might be termed a sort of, 'Pidgin' Welsh.

The specificity of my 1 abiding memory of that afternoon is restricted to a question that I must have asked my Aunt Elaine. Because, I remember my aunt saying to me as if by way of reply _ 'Mam yn cooko mushrooms'. This is the pidgin Welsh for ' …grandmother is cooking mushrooms…….'!

'Mam' was, I suppose, a term of endearment for one's grandmother. My mother's own mother (1905 - 1997) was also known to me as 'Mam'. This term is distinguishable from the term my sister and me would use for our own mother- 'Mami' was how we were both taught to, and DID, address our own mother.

But, it was sometime later that the true cause of death had been revealed pernicious anaemia! This, more than anything else, explained her frailty. Although most people in our society could be expected to live a natural lifespan of some 70 years; after all, Great Britain was a relatively wealthy country with good sanitation thanks to the endeavours of Bazalgette a century earlier, we also, as a country had had a National Health Service Years since just after cessation of WW2. Much later, when I became an undergraduate student studying pharmacy, it became clear that her death could have been postponed, Perhaps for many years. The treatment she did receive was always doomed to be in-effective. It was eating as much raw liver as could be tolerated! Nobody had yet learned that a simple, oral tablet of Cyancobalamin (nowadays, it's analogue Hydroxocobalamin) is used as the 'Magic bullet) for this 'Megaloblastic anaemia' Both are, even to this day, a simple, cheap and effective cure.

1966

This calendar year was, for my family and associates, my immediate neighbours and many people we encountered from day to day, dominated by just one event : The Welsh National Eisteddfod. An 'Eisteddfod' is a cultural gathering. It is a meeting of like minded people. It is held on a national and, international stage. It is held during the month August. Perhaps this is to assist attendance figures. After all, August it at peak of summer holiday time.

In 1966, the Eisteddfod was held in field in Margam. The field is still there and is within easy walking distance of Margam Abbey. The Bbey now stands at the very edge of Margam country Park; complete with castle. The castle itself my look very imposing. But the reality is that it is no more than just a 'folly'. It dates from the mid 19th century and the castle's original occupant was Mansel Rice Talbot, a mid-Victorian era entrepreneur. Mansel Rice Talbot became a rich man after profiting from the proceeds of photography. He was then instrumental in constructing housing development. In fact,a present area of the city of Swansea known as 'Manselton' is named after him.

The 1966 Eisteddfod was a huge attraction for my, reasonably cultured, family. It also dominated my junior school"s curriculum for the term times leading up to the August.

It had been decided by the representatives of junior's educators (The School's Authorities, its teachers and staff), that our theme for the planned appearance of my class at school, would be by way of a pageant in honour our counterparts in China! Why on earth Maoist China was chosen, one can only speculate! While it is historically true that Chairman Mao - Tse - Tung was very much alive and kicking at this time, less than 20 years after his so- called 'Cultural Revolution'

We junior schoolchildren were to to be paired; one boy with one girl. We would be clothed in uniforms typically, and apparently, as our counterparts in the real China would appear.

I could still put the name to my girl partner. I recall her being year older than I but, of course we would both have begun our schooling careers within a year of each other and would remain in the same mainstream schools until the end of our compulsory schooling years at the age of 16. Sadly, I have not seen or heard from her since leaving secondary school.

1967

I remember almost nothing from this year aside from just 2 events. The first, an exchange on the school bus. As we were very small children and as the journey to and from school was around 5 miles from Margam to Pontrhydyfen, we kind of got to know our driver and a man who used to accompany us. I guess he must have worked as the bus's 'conductor' because he always stood on or near the footplate of the guys. He would say 'Good morning' by way of greeting as each boy or girl and entered although I cannot remember him being so forthcoming with any end of day comment on the way home. He knew us all by our first names and, I guess, had an inkling on how best to deal with each child's character or foibles. For example, some girls' tendency would be to be tearful, some boys (and some girls too) were rather bellicose! Yet others never seemed to say or do anything throughout the journey whereas others would positively bound on to or off the bus at the beginning or end of the school journey. I, my sister and another boy and girl had the longest journeys. We were always first on to the bus in the mornings, and last off in the afternoons.

On 11th December it was of course, my 7th birthday. Our school bus conductor also claimed it was HIS birthday too. I think it may have been his 67th but I may be mistaken! He seemed, after all, to be VERY old so I would not have been in any position to gainsay his claim, even if I had wanted to. I remember at the time, wondering what it would be like to be that age. With hindsight, he may have been born in the late Victorian era and he would have seen 2 world wars as well as the general strike of 1926 during his lifetime.

We wished each other 'Happy Birthday' and I got off the bus at our school gate's stop. My teachers would, of course, have known it was my birthday too but as my classmates would have been engaged in making our Christmas decorations for the upcoming holiday, we had other things and tasks 'on our plates' We children were been told how to do some of the practical tasks associated with Christmas such as making our own versions of Christmas cards, arranging tinsel displays and, of course, learning and practising singing our favourite Christmas carols.

A sad occurrence which happened at some point that year was when my 'Aunty' Dorothy's fiancé was killed in an industrial accident at his place of work. Apparently, having already finished his shift for the day, he went to ask whether any of the other workers wanted any help. As a result, he was asked to access a vat of Sulphuric Acid for which he would have to use a plank of wood to gain access, He slipped while crossing the plank of wood and so he fell into the vat of acid. He suffered 80% burns and was rushed to the St Lawrence hospital in Chepstow which was the nearest specialist burns unit to his workplace.

My Aunty Dorothy went to visit him in hospital more than once, But, sadly, He died a few days later,

The second memorable event was the wedding of my Aunt Elaine. The wedding's religious ceremony took place at 'Noddfa' the independent, congregational chapel in Taibach that was the chapel attended by all members of my immediate family. The building is still there in Commercial Road, Taibach, but it has now undergone a change of use and is no longer a religious venue.

My late Aunt (1931 - 2017) aside from a few months as a married woman, had never moved outside Port Talbot to live . She was my father's only sibling, and also 11 years his junior. After her basic schooling, she got a secure job in the Research centre at port Talbot steelworks. That is what I knew of her antecedents until she met the man who would become her husband.

He too, was from Port Talbot but he already had a son of around my age at the time. I have no idea what happened to him or to his son. I would not recognise either if I saw them again.

The marriage of my aunt was characterised by allegations of improper behaviour and acts of spitefulness on my Aunt's husband's part.

They had first met at a Casino in Port Talbot and I recall my aunt being head over heels in love. But clearly, there were intra-marital problems…!

In or about 1967, I had my first encounter with football or 'Soccer' as it was popularly known.

The was a match being screened on our house's, rented, '405 lines' home TV one evening.

I remember that the action was being talked about by, what seemed to be, a man within my personal earshot, but was actually, invisible! This was perhaps the first time that I had heard the opinions of anyone who was not actually present in the room, or other space, that I happened to be occupying.

Of course; the voice was that of a TV football commentator! I wonder if, given the year, and that this was in all likelihood, a BBC broadcast, [the BBC was my parents' favourite choice of broadcasting station]. (There were, after all, only 2 choices in existence in those days; the BBC and ITV) that the man was actually, none other than Kenneth Wolstenholme?

Soccer became a focal reference point for me from that day. And I am still interested in the fortunes of my own favourite teams, the players, personalities and general hubbub that surrounds the sport, as will become apparent later on.

1968 and 1969

I still recall one notable event which happened toward the end of my school's summer term in 1968, it occurred over the days between say, 30th June, until the afternoon of 2nd July 1968. It was a heavy thunderstorm. I have since found out that this particular thunderstorm was widespread in area, enduring in it's duration and, it covered all of Southern England (and my part of South Wales too).

I recall going to bed as normal that evening. It would not have been much later than 8 in the evening I suppose. After all, there WOULD be school the next day.

The next thing I remember is being woken in the middle of the night by noise. The noise sounded rather unique. In fact, it sounded like nothing I had heard before, both in it's quality and it's intensity. Of course, it was just the thunder and the sound of the raindrops and hailstones clattering against the pavements, the roads, and anything attached to, or on to them.

But, it disturbed me. I remember calling out for my parents in fear. My father came into my bedroom and we both went, at my father's invitation, to look out of a side of house, upstairs window. My father mumbled something about 'It (being) down Pyle way'. Those familiar with this area of South Wales will know that Pyle is small town about 5 miles to the east of Port Talbot. I looked out of the window and saw a series of lightning bolts falling from the sky towards the ground. I must have seen 2 or 3 in quick succession and, all seemed to start from approximately, the same starting point in the night's black sky.

The following day, everyone seemed to be talking about the storm, the intensity of the rain and hail and the frequency of he lightning. At school, on the bus to school, while at school, or even the total strangers conversing with each other on the street. I heard some of the adults in our area describing it as being similar to the noise of the air raids during WW2. As the day wore on, more black clouds appeared; the thunder was back!

I then saw one of the most amazing sights that I have ever experienced. It remains with my to this day!

I was idly gazing out of my classroom's window. The window faced the tallest mountain in the whole of the county of Glamorgan, known as 'Foel Fynyddau'.

I then saw a pink, translucent, sort of curtain appearing to tumble all the way down my facing side of the mountain. The appearance only lasted a few seconds but was followed in short order by an amazing, and very loud, clap of thunder.

It was no illusion.

But the pink translucency may have been no more than 'sheet' lightning, that is, a reflection from a more distant lightning bolt off either of the faces of 'Penrhys' or 'Penhydd' mountains.

In fact our local newspaper, init's 2nd July 1968 described the previous night as a 'night of terror and havoc' and drew a parallel with events of the wartime air raids which would still have been relatively fresh in the memories of those who had lived through it.

I recall the consistent accounts given by my classmates the following day (2nd July). It seemed that absolutely nobody had managed to sleep through the thunderstorm.

Now, and with the benefit of many years hindsight, I just remember the whole experience as being quite spooky.

A postscript to the storm was that on the 2nd July, my class teacher told us children that our school's pet goldfish had died overnight and had, in fact, been found dead when the teachers had arrived for work that morning. By way of explanation, our teacher speculated that the previous night's thunderstorm had been so violent, that our goldfish died as a result!

Another chain of events, though, of course, not one to which I was in any way a personal witness, occurred during December of 1968. It was NASAs 'Apollo 8' moon mission.

This marked the 1st time in history that man, not only had escaped the force of Earth's gravitational hold, (that feat had been accomplished several times since Yuri Gagarin's flight in 'Vostok' 1 in 1957), but that mankind had now succeeded in flying to a truly extraterrestrial body; (the Moon).

There had been prominent commentary and build up on both UK TV networks: the BBC and ITV. Aa a family, we preferred the BBCs coverage throughout the Apollo programme..

Headed by the astronomer Patrick Moore as technical expert and James Burke as the journalistic/public's representative, a great deal of broadcast time was devoted to the event. From lift off using the gigantic 'Saturn 5' rocket; the TV pictures of the 365 foot high vehicle resting quietly pre lift off against the massive launch apparatus situated in the Florida swamps at Cape Canaveral at launchpad 39A! Through lift off procedure itself with the seemingly relentless countdown TV pictures of the rocket climbing gracefully until it escaped the gravitational pull of Earth until it's propulsive force equalled the pull of the Earth's gravity force. This meant that the spacecraft was in earth orbit. There would then be a further manoeuvre - a rocket burn to propel Apollo 8 moon bound. The spacecraft would then be captured by the gravitational pull of the moon itself. The moon is only around one-fifth of that of the Earth, but, lunar orbit would then be attained. The 3 astronauts aboard, the mission's commander; Frank Borman (1928 - 2023),the Lunar module pilot; James Lovell (born 1928), and Command module pilot; William Anders (1930 - 2024), then themselves orbited the moon, taking photographs of both nearside and, the never been seen from anywhere on Earth before, the far side!

At the intersection point, one of the most iconic photographs of the vista was taken; 'Earthrise'! Man could, for the first time in history see his own planet rising above his visual horizon!

This all happened very near to Christmas Day itself. I recall that, in Margam, we were having a clear, cold, frosty, moonlit night one night very close to Christmas Day. My father and me stepped outside the warmth and comfort of our house. My father looked at the bright moon, shining brightly out of the crystal clear sky, turned to me, and said'Isn't it amazing that there are men travelling around that (the Moon) right at this minute, as we are looking at it' For a man or boy whose only real, documented account of the wonders of reality and the universe would have been a Jules Verne story. For my father's part, this sort of sight would have been one that none of his contemporaries, nor his ancestors, could possibly have envisaged. Science fiction had truly met science fact!

The extensive TV coverage of the mission lasted until the spacecraft's successful return to Earth via it's Command Module's 'Splashdown' in the Pacific Ocean; at which point normal TV schedules were re-established.

That, of course, meant there was plenty to discuss at school for myself and the other boys (it did seem to be far more of a talking point for us boys than it was for any of the girls!

I can't explain this! Why, when we're taught that all human beings, regardless of gender, are of equal value, all girls or women were considered as the 'gentler' sex and were also being considered as incapable of many occupations as a result during the 1960s, much of the'79s, less of the '80s and '90s, and almost none of the 35 plus years since.

But I was transfixed by the 'Apollo' concept and its missions!

I simply wanted to know and learn more and more. I became a fan of space travel. In fact, I was a faithful devotee of the 'Apollo' programme and it's successors ('Skylab', 'The Space shuttle' for the USA) and 'Soyuz' and 'Salyut' for their technological and bitter political rivals, the (then termed) USSR.

In 1968, my mother had begun learning to drive. She was, by then, already 42 years of age - rather late to be learning a new technical skill in the minds of the people she consulted on the matter. Contemporaneously, my father, who was now himself, 48 years old wanted, to learn to drive, himself. I suspect he just did not want to be out done. After all, he would not have NEEDED to be able to drive, his workplace was only a 10 to 15 minute gentle walk from our house. But the ability to drive would be a boon for my mother's career. Since qualifying as a nurse during the time of the Swansea blitz in 1943, her ability to drive her own, private car could, and would, open the door to her becoming a district nurse. She was duly appointed and remained 'On the district' until the mid 1970s. My father, not to be outdone, began learning to drive in around 1968. He duly passed his drivers test too, and so we, as a family, were now fully mobile and able to drive out, and back to distant destinations, whenever the fancy took us, and for whatever reason.

Sunday afternoons in particular, were occasions the my father and mother would share duties to drive us to places of interest, to visit family friends or relations and to travel to the funfair at Porthcawl or my mother's large family in Manselton, Swansea and the like.

It was around this time that another literary genre became an interest; Horror movies!

In those days, a weekly trip to one of the local cinemas would customarily be taken.

There were 2 cinemas in Port Talbot - the 'Odeon' at the bottom end of Forge Road, almost at the junction with Station Road and The 'Plaza' (still there to this day) in Station Road opposite the main line railway station.

It never ceased as a source of wonderment to me that, having gone to a cinema to see a screening of a movie classed as being fit for universal exhibition; there always seemed to be trailers (of seemingly lengthy duration) advertising a violent film, a horror film or a film with romance as a central theme. In 1968, Roger's and Hammerstein's 'The Sound of Music' was still on display, as was 'Oliver' starring Ron Moody and Oliver Reed, There was 'Chitty, Chitty, Bang, Bang' an onomatopoeically titled story of a family saloon car, but, one that could fly!

But there were also pre exhibition trailers for such films as 'Dracula has risen from the Grave', 'Frankenstein created woman' and, 'Frankenstein must be destroyed'

Why were they there? Why did someone, or something want to interfere with my enjoyment of a light comedy, musical or other genre of film interesting to a 7 year old boy, to cause distress or awe?

I was fascinated. And that sense of fascination has never left me,

1969 was the year of the 'Apollo' program's zenith : the first successful moon landing. Achieved in the July, it was held to be a justification of the vast sums the USA, as a nation were investing in the space program.

Meanwhile, The US government's goals and policies were, by no means going without criticism from its own electorate.

The year's space missions ; consecutively numbered 9 and 10. Occurred in, respectively, the March and the May of that year. Talk was; if they were successful, the 1st moon landing itself would occur in July.

I was in a phase of heightened excitement as the school term, and academic year progressed.

My form teacher, a young woman called Lynwen Samuel, appeared to be engaged with the interest in the 'Apollo' program herself. After all, would it not have given her, as a very young member of the teaching profession, something topical to address her earliest classes with?

I sensed that I was becoming something of a 'one trick pony' at school. I still had 2 academic years to finish before leaving for secondary school. I was beginning to gain weight, I was not particularly athletic, was not being asked to represent the school in its soccer matches or other outdoor pursuits aside from the introduction to the piano that my father had afforded me at home, and my still relatively good physical stamina level, I was by no means the 'Star' of my class or year at anything. Some of my classmates, for instance, were skilful soccer players, others sang or played musical instruments, but not me!

In my case, and by reason of my having taken an extra 2 years to do my 'A' Level exams, I eventually left school in 1979 at the age of 18 years and a few months.

Having been fortunate enough to have attained this academic level, and not having decided to join any of the armed services, the police or fire service, I became a University undergraduate that same year.

The last day of the 1979 academic year was, sadly, the last time I saw, or spoke to, many of the names and faces amongst those I had schooled with. I sometimes wonder what became of those school friends. A relatively small number, I know. One or two have become famous and, in at least 1 case, infamous!

But, back to the original chronology and continuing from the end of 1969:

1970

Nominally, the start of a new decade. Or was it? I suppose it depends on the method you use to compute time!

That, in turn, depends on whether you consider 'Zero' to be a number or a numberless concept.

If you DO consider zero to be a discreet number, then the year 1960 (my birth year) would have to have marked the very beginning of the 1960s. Similarly, 1950 was the beginning of the 1950s, 1940 of the 1940s and so on.

But if zero means exactly that: Nothing, then the 1970s couldn't have actually begun until 1st January 1971!

The '1960s' would have begun on 1st January 1961 and so on, 'ad infinitum' !

Similarly, the majority of the word's population seemed to consider that the new millennium started at mid night on New Year's Day a.d. 2000. Certainly, that's when all the celebrations and fireworks displays suggested we had entered the new millennium and the 'Noughties'. The true reality is that, we should have waited until midnight on 1st January 2021!

But, I digress:

In common with the vest majority of the population, we considered the seventies to be the dawn of a new era, a new decade. Goodbye the 'Swinging sixties' Goodbye the brightly coloured clothing, and goodbye to the extravagant long hairstyles for men. In common with most people, that new epoch and the new styles of living were deemed to have happened on 1 January 1970.

Having written the above account and also, perhaps being on the mildly autistic spectrum, I considered it to be important; all this fuss about a new decade, the new decade, new epoch and anything that went with it all seemed to happen with a whimper, as opposed to a bang!

I would still have to attend school on the 1st day of the spring term; it would still be dark early, therefore dark when we left at the end of the school day, there would still be the sense of misery (on the one hand) and anticipation (on the other). Perhaps the realisation of some of my personal ambitions would be just around the corner. Perhaps there would be a dynamic new teacher to take our classes. Or a new boy or girl in my class this year?

With digression, I don't think that there were. But hey! that surely is not the point in question, is it?

Well no!

Regardless of what went on in others' houses, there would always be SOMETHING happening. Something to talk about in class or at home; something to do in spare time, something to distinguish this new year, and decade from the past.

Indeed there was!

1971

On 15th February 1971, Britain 'went decimal'!

True, we the public had fair warning that things would never be the same again from that date.

A series of TV adverts with short, but attractive and memorable musical 'Jingles' or slogans peppered the airwaves. There was much discussion about the changes to the coinage at school.

We learned, along withe rest of the nation, young or old, about the new Coins (the 50p piece, the 10p piece) the discontinuation of paper pound and 10 shilling notes, loss of the old threepenny and sixpenny 'bits' and, most importantly, how to calculate the conversion factors between the 'old' and 'new' currencies.

As the 15th February 1971 drew closer and close, attempts were made to divest ourselves of coinage that would soon be unusable as currency. While it was right, and prudent, that the authorities had allowed grace periods whereby old coinage could be exchanged at post offices, our local post office was unlikely to have the capacity to deal with large sums.

Therefore, as 1970 became 1971, many of the British public became preoccupied with official advice, expressed in catchy and rhythmical 'jingles' that '£1 = 100 new pennies; 100 new pence to the pound' 'Use your old pennies in sixpenny lots', and the like.

The basic conversion factor was that 1 new penny - still in circulation today, over 50 years later, was equivalent to 'tuppence ha'penny' of old money (you know, the large, flat, circular old coins made of bronze) that, with inflation, were becoming of lower and lower value and with less intrinsic spending power, as time went on.

I still remember the big day itself! After school, our local shops were overwhelmed with people trying not only to still be getting rid of their old coinage, but to be among the first people to acquire the 'new coins'.

Much time was spent in shop queues while people bringing the shopkeepers large consignments of e.g. old pennies, old threepenny or sixpenny 'bits' so they would swap for the equivalent in decimal currency. The poor shopkeepers, many of whom were simply running family businesses must have felt rather overwhelmed!

Of course, the government had allowed sufficient leeway for the change to occur without financial loss to anyone. In particular, it had been decided in certain media outlets, that 'old' people would be especially vulnerable to any sharp practices by traders. How patronising! But we youngsters seemed to be immune from the effects of the changes.

How satisfying it was, for example, to be able to swap one of those old, crumpled 10 shilling notes for a bright, newly minted, gleaming, shiny and a truly mint-condition 50p piece!

Fears of the patronisingly designated 'old or elderly' people being 'fiddled' by unscrupulous traders were proving unfounded, and Britain, as a whole, seemed to quickly adapt to the new regime.

As 1971 progressed, the Apollo moon landing program proceeded forwards after the near disaster of Apollo 13 in April 1970 and duly reached beyond the 18 month flight postponements that had initially been announced by NASA with Apollo14 eventually launching successfully in February 1971 and Apollo 15 launching in the July of 1971.

Some of the highlights for me, as an aficionado, were the attempt to play golf on the moon's surface were made by one of the Apollo 14 astronauts, Alan Shepherd. A piece of the flight's equipment was used as an ersatz club. He produced a golf ball which he had sneaked on to the moon mission at lift off from Cape Canaveral, produced it from his spacesuit after landing on the moon and drove a ball across the lunar surface! Generous man; he did not claim a hole in one!

Apollo 15 in July 1971 was the 1st spacecraft to land on the moon carrying a 'Lunar Rover Vehicle' (LRV). This allowed the 2 landing members of the 3 man crew to drive across the lunar surface, rather bumpily, as it turned out, but further significant progress for the American space project nevertheless. The LRV was also carried on the 2 subsequent moon landings in 1972 namely Apollos 16 and 17.

That brought to an end, mankind's first hand exploration of the moon. Man is not due to return to the moon until 2026 (at the earliest).

But, to return to the year 1970 for a final moment, on 11th December, I attained the grand age of 10 years. The whole of that week, a gas fitter had been at our family's home in Margam in order to install new gas central heating equipment.

This would be a vast improvement on our cumbersome and, by today's standards, dirty, old coal fires.

The coal fire's flue pipe was confined to the TV lounge room in our 3 bedroomed, semi detached house. Therefore it's heat only truly benefitted that 1 room. all the upstairs rooms, including both the house's 2 main bedrooms, bathroom, and a small 'Box room' on the upstairs floors always seemed to be stone cold in winter! This was particularly noticeable and acute on cold winter mornings when often, the inside glass panes would be frosted with ice! It was my mother's job to light the house's fire each morning. Even at my young age, I sympathised with her. She would have to rise from under the bedclothes each morning, troop downstairs, ensure enough coal was in a freshly cleaned grate (the actual cleaning of the grate was customarily done last thing at night by one or other of my parents). Having judged the amount of coal that would be needed to keep the house warm for our waking hours, a supply of chopped wood would also be necessary as kindling. Toward the end of this soon to be defunct arrangment, my parents would also buy 'Firelighters' from our local hardware store in Tollgate Road, Margam. I never found out what the were made of, but they were a white, waxy substance that the manufacturer claimed would distribute the heat from the lumps of coal and sticks of kindling less in - efficiently.

So, what a relief to our family when, on 11th December 1970, our family's new gas central heating equipment was finally installed. The fireplace itself remained in our lounge. But now, a series of convection/conduction pipes also ensured that every room in the house could also be supplied with heat, if necessary.

The converse was also true. So, if it was considered that any room was not in need of immediate heat, the radiator for that room could be temporarily turned off.

Also on this memorable day, I got the birthday present of my dreams: a CHEMISTRY SET! Specifically, a 'Fisher Price's CHEMISTRY SET.

With my father being an experienced chemistry technician at the local steel plant, I would be able to follow in my his footsteps and become a chemist myself when I grew up. My father's chemistry manuals were handily still kept in the house. I remember them as small and compact books published by a firm known as 'Balliere, Tindall & Cox'. I couldn't wait….! These small, brown, hardback volumes were packed full of interesting information about chemistry. The headings in the manual also included one on 'Physiological Action' of each entry! So, even years before was ready, I knew why pure Phosphorus was caustic, why Potassium Cyanide was soo toxic and why Arsenic was so insidious as a poison! I must have spent many hours in bed, reading snippets of knowledge every night, before sleep, reading about things that would eventually be useful in my future career as a pharmacist. But, what would I become? Would I eventually be an academic?, a doctor?, a chemist?, a professor? I couldn't possibly have known at just 10 years of age. But, I had, even then, made up my mind that I would do something worthwhile.

What I DID do between the ages of 10 and my eventual career was due, in large part to events that befell me over the next 5 years.

1971

I remember spending almost the entirely of that warm, dry summer holiday period in Aberavon beach taking advantage of the warm sea. At that time, it was only just becoming affected by the 'Torrey Canyon' Oil tanker disaster of 1967. The resulting leaks of crude oil had not yet fully made their way from the north-west Atlantic Ocean to the sandy beach at Aberavon. It would take another few years, until the characteristic cow-pat like blobs of dirty - looking oil would make it on to the sands of Atlantic facing beaches.

Another memory concerned the almost perpetual smiles my father was wearing as a result of news updates from the successful British Lions rugby tour of New Zealand. I particularly recall his leaps of joy in our house when it became that, having won the 3rd test, the Lions were not able to be overtaken in the 4 match series. But also when they drew the final test a fortnight later which meant they had won the overall series by 2 matches to 1, with one drawn.

I also recall another heavy thunderstorm during the night of 30th July. This one seemed to have come from nowhere, unlike the one just over 3 years earlier which had been presaged by the depositing of orangey-red coloured atmospheric dust which, for several days had been covering the roads and any vehicles on them. Apparently, this orange-red dust had been blown high into the Earth's atmosphere, was made up of fine, Saharan sand grains and, when the conditions had been right, precipitated the aforementioned storm of 1st and 2nd July 1968.

1972

That year was to mark the end of my time at a junior school. My parents had decided the my best choice would be to follow a path that favoured a bi-lingual path. The respective languages were, in my case (as for almost all boys and girls in South Wales, English (of course!) and Welsh. The advantages of retaining the same path in secondary school as in junior school were easily manifest:- familiarity with the other boys and girls from my junior school, continuity, and companionship. The converse choice for my parents was to send me to Glanafan school in Port Talbot town centre. This would be much nearer to my home address, but I would know absolutely nobody on day one and, the school did not have as strong a Welsh department as the eventual choice,namely, the bi- lingual 'Ysgol Gyfun' in a little village called Ystalyfera. The noun translates directly into the English language as; Ystalyfera 'Comprehensive' School.

The 'Comprehensive system of schooling had been favoured by the then legislators (Harold Wilson's socialist 'Labour' government) to the previous system of 'Grammar' schools, for the academically brighter prospects, and 'Secondary modern' schools for those pupils for whom academic study would be of lesser importance to acquiring practical, or artisan skills. In those days, the choices would also import considerations based on the prospective pupil's gender, Boys would have a choice of studying woodwork, metalwork, plant and animal husbandry and the like, The girls would be expected to take cookery, needlework and, the domestic sciences lessons; based on their own anticipated future prospects.

All pupils in the new 'Comprehensive' schools would take the 3 R/s subjects, so English lessons were compulsory, as was Maths. Then would come the academic subjects such as Geography and History, music, both theoretical and practical, Finally were ranked the quasi-academic, or— 'artisan' pursuits such as Art and team or individual sports and games, music, drama and the like.

Of course, I looked forward, very much to my formal lessons in science subjects. Chemistry (like dad!), Physics and Biology.

At the same time, I was also keeping up with my piano lessons.

After all, hadn't I achieved a 'Distinction' assessment for my recent Royal College of Music Grade 1 (introductory) exam. I had scored 97 marks out of possible 100 in the combined theory and practical exam!

I liked sports too, but was not particularly good at them.

I strongly suspect, with the benefit of over 50 years of hindsight; it was around this time, in the early part of the 1970s, that I first showed signs of my Type I (insulin dependant) diabetes: - I had started feeling increasingly hungry and began to put on a lot of body weight around my midriff area. In short, I was becoming 'FAT'!

I had, though, always enjoyed my food. Even our Sunday lunches with their rotation of lamb, beef, pork or chicken on a roughly, weekly basis during th months, were always gobbled up. There would also be vegetables on offer, particularly carrots, swede, parsnips and potatoes with, usually, a helping of either cabbage or cauliflower as 'greens'. I suspected that our family had, in general terms, a healthier diet than many of my classmates. Talk of what we had had to eat over school term time weekends revealed that many classmates were subjected to living off 'SPAM', Chopped ham with Pork, chips and such confections as Bird's 'Angel Delight' (which I could never abide!).

But now, I would crave multiple helpings of absolutely EVERYTHING!

It was no wonder I got fat!

So hungry was I, than I used to raid the fridge every evening after school. It got so bad, that I must have been spending at least as much time at the fridge door in our family's kitchen as I did elsewhere in the house.

My favourite 'snack' was great big lumps of (usually) Cheddar Cheese. If the family was low on Cheddar cheese, normally because It was I, who was eating far too much of it, I would find some other high energy replacement from the fridge.

I now understand that that would be because my body was incapable of properly utilising the nutrients in food, due to my deficit of the hormone, Insulin.

As a result, between the year 1971 and late 1974 I was simply a fat glutton!

With hindsight, 1973 was the last full year where I could live an untrammelled lifestyle.

I can still remember that our family's annual summer holidays were spent away at Ilfracombe (again!) and various day-trips to places like Caswell Bay and Oxwich in the Gower peninsula.

I suppose that an enduring bright spot' from this entire era arose from my always having been quite physically fit. I liked swimming, I had stamina in large quantities, I loved walking and climbing. But, I WAS too fat. My schoolmates, including several of my teachers, even began to refer to me as 'Tank'.

That was all to change the following year. Specifically, in the days surrounding 30th October 1974.

That week was half term week at school. In those days, the mid term or 'half-term' holidays (in both autumn and spring) were over only 3 days instead of being over the entire week, like the are today.

We pupils had to attend our school classes on the Mondays and Tuesdays but then, were off school for the Wednesdays, Thursdays and Fridays of each half term weeks.

This half term appeared to begin as usual for me. But now there was a change: I was becoming increasingly thirsty! These sensations of feeling thirsty gradually overwhelmed me and it seemed as if I was now ALWAYS feeling thirsty! The remedy for these feelings was un-surprising; I felt the need to keep drinking fluids! This is what I did, it was just that now, I had no choice.

Any medical doctor, nurse or even student doctors will term this condition as one of 'poly - dypsia'. I had developed 'polydypsia' in excess!

Of course, the payback for so much fluid intake was frequent urination! This caused me to become dehydrated which, of course, set up a biological 'positive feedback' loop to my body.

This was exactly what was happening to me over the autumn half term holiday in 1974.

I could not go longer than about 20 minutes at a time, without passing water!

I had found myself complaining to my mother (herself, a qualified nurse) over a few days, of this un- avoidable need to pass water. As an 'SRN' (State Registered Nurse), I would always naturally defer to greater her knowledge and expertise on all medical matters. She had, after all, trained in nursing from the age of 14 at the old Swansea Hospital, and had qualified with her full practising rights in 1943. She remembered, at first hand, the awful few nights marking the Swansea 'Blitz' when the German 'Luftwaffe' terrorised both my mother's home residential area of Morriston AND my father's and his parents and little sister's house in Brombil Street, Margam in a series of enemy air raids that had resulted in them still being talked about some 3 decades later. As the hostilities abated, my mother had also had trained as a midwife, and then, bolstered by the fact of her having passed her UK driver's test in 1967at her second attempt , she had also become a 'District' nurse. During her working days, she could find herself being 'on-call' at any time of the day or night.

Much of her weekly roster in the mid 1970s consisted, typically, of sessions at various medical practices, at Doctor's surgeries, and, the ability to confer with or offer advice to, patients in their own homes as part of 'The District' duties.

So, by autumn 1974, she was a very experienced nurse having, by then, been in practice for over 30 years.

She decided to take a sample of my urine to work at 'The Mount Surgery' that morning, so that it could be analysed. I have no idea whether this was her rostered place of work for that day or whether it was something done using her own initiative under the family's comity with me, as her son.. I recall it being during the middle of the week, I believe, it may have been a Thursday

In those now far off, days, our school half term breaks only lasted 3 days rather than the full 5 working weekdays of today's schoolchildren.

I suppose that I myself had been feeling sub-par for at least a few days. On reflection, I was not my usual, bright, bubbly, active self and so found myself confined to the family's house in rather dark and grey, but, as I recall, dry conditions.

Normally, the fact of school holidays and the prevailing half-decent weather conditions would have been enough for me to go and kick a football around or go walking or swimming or, at any rate, get out of the house. But I wasn't really feeling 'up to it' this time 'round.

Imagine my surprise when my mother turned up at our house during the middle of the day. She had NEVER, to my knowledge, done that before and certainly, not while I was in the house too. ! At that point however, I confess I had quite forgotten her leaving the house to attend work at all that day!

By her demeanour however, I had an instinct that something was wrong,

I can't now remember which of us spoke first but I DO remember her using the phrase, '….. urine was full of sugar……'.

My blood chilled on hearing that!

I knew there was some bad news on the way because, I recall that my father's favourite piano pupil, a girl that lived very close to us, had been diagnosed with Type 1 diabetes only a few years earlier.

I had gleaned, as a result, that her fate involved her having to have injections every day. This seemed to me to be a horrible curse and. because she continued to be my father's piano pupil and had, apparently, been continuing at her school, her having to endure daily injections seemed to me to be a disproportionate outcome for her, if not, downright cruel! I had picked up that the injections were of a substance called 'Insulin'. It was at that point that the word 'Insulin' entered my vocabulary. So, now, in late 1974, 'Insulin' was a prospect that filled me with a measure of dread, fear and despair.

My mother told me that, although she had to return to the Mount surgery for her afternoon shift, an appointment had already been put in place for me to accompany her to an evening surgery appointment with my registered GP, a Doctor named Claude Thomas.

My mother and me both attended as arranged.

I still remember my mood as being one of bewilderment more than anything else. My mother had, wisely, advised me not to eat or drink ANYTHING at least until we had been for the appointment and returned home!

Imagine! I would not be able to engage in my favourite latest occupation of 'pigging out' that afternoon. So, my first thoughts as a 13 year old boy were along the lines of 'what a waste of an afternoon!'.

When we got to the appointment, I learned that, at least I would be seeing a partner, in Dr Thomas, who would be a familiar face.

I remember that he appeared to have pre-armed himself with what appeared to be paperback books. There was more than 1 such book, but the one that sticks in my mind was coloured a horrible, light yellow or buff shade with plain, black writing.

It turned out to be a book containing Diet sheets, some practical advice such as how much bread by weight comprised a 'slice', recipes incorporating low calorie and/or low sugar comestibles and lists of the corresponding calorie, carbohydrate, fat and protein contents of a large range of common foodstuffs. These foodstuffs included the familiar green vegetables, the citrus fruits, the meats and the grains, most of which foodstuffs I was already familiar with through our family's typical dietary intake of the day. What was NOT included were proprietary foods like 'Spam' or 'BirdsEye's range of flavoured jellies and the like. But the generic equivalent of many WERE included, For example, 'chopped ham and pork' was widely available in shops and supermarkets. Very usefully, the diet sheets' pages also reinforced many aspects of knowledge which formed part of to my study, and my preparations for my school's Biology 'O' level syllabus which subject I enjoyed, and looked forward to learning from the beginning of the following academic year (which would be 1975/6). I could already tell that I had a preference for the science subjects over the arts subjects. So Chemistry, Biology and, to a lesser extent, Physics were my favourites. The only real exception to this generality was Music which I also loved and where my school had a very well equipped music department.

Attempts had been made by the author, a sometime consultant physician based at University College Hospital in London (UCH) at to rank these Diabetic diets into, so-called 'Free' foods. Free foods were those which would have a negligible or very low, 'Glycaemic index', followed by the types of food that had some restrictions on what, or the amount, it was permissible to eat. Examples could include un-thickened, stocks such as 'Marmite' or 'Oxo'. Finally, there were the foodstuffs that were either severely restricted or outright 'disallowed'. Typical 'Free' foods were Lettuce and cabbage, moderately restricted were most red meats, beans or pulses, more restricted included corn and 'Root' vegetables such as carrots, swede and parsnips. The totally disallowed foods were refined sugar itself sweets, any thing made using refined sugar such as chocolates and sugary drinks like ordinary Lemonade, cherry-ade, Limeade and the like.

That being the case, it made things like going out with friends, visiting cafes, sweet shops and restaurants that much more difficult. In contrast to today, where virtually all comestibles are available in sugar - free options, the only safe option was to ask for tap water or bottled water! In fact 'Soda' water became a staple of mine. With time, I learned to use soda water as a drink mixer so that imparted 'fizz' to drinks of orange, lemon or lime squash. One still had to be careful because of course, the supermarket fruit squashes were themselves mainly sweetened with sugar!

Heeding my Doctors' advice, I lost a large amount of weight VERY quickly. I went from weighing 11 and a half stones to just 9 and a half stones over the 4 or 5 days before I was then due back at school to finish that term's classes.

Imagine the reaction of most of my school-friends when they saw the effect on my new physique!

For a start; was it now going to be accurate to refer to me as 'Tank'?

(In fact, the old Nickname stuck for much longer than it ought to have done). In point of fact, it only petered out once I had left the junior's section of school. By the time of my 'A' level years (1977 -79), hardly anybody would continue to refer to me as 'Tank'.

Not that long after my diagnosis in 1974 (but actually, by no later than some point in 1975) a significant development to the availability and palatability of such 'diabetic' products was introduced; The 'Saccharin' tablets. By which I mean PALATABLE Saccharin tablets. The substance 'Saccharin' had been known about for several decades before then. In fact, it is a substance that is extracted by chemical modification of certain species of seaweeds. Saccharin was even available from just after the war years, that is, from the late 1940s and 1950s. It's advantage was that it was a cheap commodity. I remember that drums containing hundreds of (very small sized) tablets could be purchased at reasonable prices.

I enjoyed my time at school too now that I was slimmer and physically fitter. I appreciated that I had been unusually sluggish immediately prior to my diagnosis. But now, I was able to be be more outgoing, more confident and more active as a person. This was just as I remembered my character of old, at the years and times prior to, say, 1973.

It did have a practical disadvantage. prior to the late 1970s, the commercially available tablets had a bitter and 'metallic' aftertaste. So they were far from perfect for frequent, daily use

As a digression, Compare this situation with today, where a sugar free variety of practically every soft drink are available from supermarkets, artificial sweeteners such as 'Aspartame' are almost ubiquitous in a variety of formulations to suit consumers' needs. And the shelves of our supermarkets are stacked with 'low calorie' and 'sugar - free' options of virtually everything. 'Bitter or metallic' aftertastes are pretty much now a thing of the past. And thankfully, they have largely been consigned to the dustbin of history.

The wheel of consumer preferences seems nowadays to have turned half circle. These days, I notice that the supermarket's shelves are stacked as much with the so called 'Free From' products than with the age old staples themselves! So, the low or free-from sugar and salt products are, perhaps, the natural by-product of this trend.

Overall, this last half century (since 1974/5) has seen vast improvements to, not just, public health itself, but to people's ATTITUDES to public health. It is no longer 'cool' to smoke tobacco products for example. But, non combustible Nicotine containing products are replacing the old cigarettes, cigars and pipes as acceptable drug delivery vehicles.

1975

As my Type 1 diabetic condition was becoming more familiar to me personally, it also had a corresponding effect on my immediate family members, my schoolmates and the teachers.

1976

The first thing that I remember, in retrospect, about the year 1976, was being given the chance to go on a lengthy school trip. To Belgium, of all places!

It's length was a whole week, and it took place sometime during the long summer holidays. I believe it must have been in the 3rd week of July. Because, as a cricket fan, I remember it overlapped with the dates of the 4th test of the England v West Indies series. There being no internet, or mobile phone service in those days, if one wanted to know the latest score or the general match situation, one would either have had to phone home or a knowledgeable friend (too expensive), or, buy an English newspaper(the ones on sale in the shops were always a day or two behind so, were out of date!). England had been heavily defeated in the 3rd test, but were still in the game during the first few days of the 4th, which was the point at which we departed for Belgium. So the exact date would have been somewhere around the 25th, 26th or 27th of July.

The trip was led by one of the school's teachers that I was not personally familiar with. He had been on military service during WW2 and, from memory, taught 'General studies' and, possibly, wood, or metal work to the secondary modern stream pupils at school

So I, as a grammar stream pupil, had never before encountered him in class.

I recall that he was very efficient and organised as befits, I suppose, an ex military man. That impression was bolstered in my mind by the fact that he had a ram-rod, straight back and always, an upright stance.

We, as the touring/visiting pupils were based in a town called 'Bredene' (pronounced 'Brea-din'). It turned out to be a North Sea seaside resort. As such, it had all the familiar embellishments that would be expected in British seaside resorts, such as; Candy-Floss stalls, souvenir shops, a Fairground, slot machines and, also having the usual types of rides such as a 'Ghost Train' and 'Dodgem' - car rinks.

There were also plenty of things to eat! The Belgians seemed very keen on 2 types of dietary treats in contrast to the boiled-sweets or the many varieties of chocolates we had been used to in the UK.: Firstly, 'Chips', in particular, the chipped, fried and in the un-processed white potato sense rather than the, seemingly ubiquitous 'French Fries' that, today, one expects from, for example, any MacDonalds or 'KFC' outlet. They were cooked there and then and were 'red' hot on being served! I recall that I would need to let my portion cool for seemingly, ages, before it was safe to even think about putting one in my mouth!

The second type of culinary treat were known as 'Waffles'. Again, these were concocted form of fried, white, potatoes, but this time, the product was presented in a lattice form. One seemed to be able to get quite ornate lattices depending on how much one was willing to pay!

As we pupils were, by now, in our 15th and 16th years of age, there was also the availability of alcohol, in the form of beer (or 'Lager' in the UK sense).

Seemingly, none of the resort's vendors bothered to ask anyone for our 'I.D', with just ONE exception (don't worry - It wasn't me!). It was a girl from amongst our group. She always seemed to be being asked for her identity. I didn't know her personally. I don't think she was part of my year, so maybe she WAS under age at the time. But, in which case, how did she come to be on our trip in the first place? One morning, we were all told that she had had to spend the previous night in prison! I don't know if this was true but it didn't seem to spoil anyone else's school trip and so, will probably always constitute one of life's little mysteries!

There was also the availability of cigarettes. A few of my fellow pupils seemed already, to be regular smokers, many others were prepared to try smoking and, of those, a number could always seem to come up with a justification for 'lighting up'. Common ones included 'Oh, I'm only trying it', 'Oh, it's only one' or, 'Oh, it's my first one ever'. I didn't smoke at all in those days and so, didn't submit to whatever blandishments tobacco smoking may have been able to offer!

By later in 1976, and bolstered by my now permanent 'slim - line' self, I was beginning to leave my childhood ways very much in my past. I don't think I had yet started shaving every day, but I was having sexual feelings for some of my contemporary school fiends, all girls, and definitely knew that I would be heterosexual. My voice was deepening and I remember one occasion when I suggested to my Father that I could come and sing with the tenor or bass sections at my father's weekly rehearsals with the 'Afan Municipal Choir'.

When it came to our school's Michaelmas term, I recall that there were also preparations for a forthcoming performance of '.

Perhaps because of my parents' affinity to choral music singing, I occasionally had been allowed to accompany my father to rehearsals.

A new, indoor, shopping mall was on the verge of opening in Port Talbot and there was to be a choral performance held there to celebrate the opening date in October of 1976. I guess the first actual 'open' date must have been between mid October and Christmas itself. The precise date would be chosen so that the venue and the soloists' availabilities could be confirmed, the event's tickets printed and for adequate publicity to be given for the event. The Afan Municipal Choir was booked to perform. All I remember about the preparation was listening to my father's endless playing of our family's piano as part of his personal preparation for the event.

So, by the time of the performance, I was familiar with the basses part for the choruses and so

I had also, previously, been able to able in at a public performance of the 'Messiah' in December 1975. That time, it had been held at one of the larger Christian, independent chapels in Port Talbot; It was known as 'Tabernacle Newydd' or 'New' Tabernacle. The building still stands (in Forge Road) but it has been deserted since the early 1990s which is when the last of it's regular worshippers died and, the building is now, sadly, derelict.

But back to my memories of 1976 and turning to the summer sports as a spectator. The West Indies team was to tour England having themselves just been heavily beaten by 5 - 1 in a 6 match test series in Australia.

In the build-up and in the early days of the tour, the West Indies team was not generally thought to have a significant chance of doing well.

This gave rise to a (now infamous) interview given by Tony Greig to the BBC on the corporation's 'Sportsnight with Coleman' TV programme which was broadcast on the tour's eve.

My own modest musical experiences were enhanced when I persuaded my school's music teacher that I was a fit person to join the school's choir. I cannot remember ever having to audition. But I suppose I must have done so , for I found myself, somewhat alone amongst the majority of my classmates, singing in the Bass section of the choir at the school's landmark performance of Vivaldi's 'Gloria' which took place at the Brangwyn Hall in late 1976. It was held there in Swansea with some very able musicians and singers among my fellow pupils at the school. . Several of my school contemporaries have since gone onto have careers as professional musicians, actors and actresses.

I was pleased to have been able to join the school's choir because, along with not just my struggles with autism, but with my personal reputation being somewhat in tatters following the upheaval of being fairly newly diagnosed with Type 1 diabetes, I guess I may have, perhaps, unfairly, been regarded as being a bit of a 'ne'er-do-well' by those who knew me.

1976 was my 3rd Christmas as a diabetic. And as I felt I was being progressively more able to adjust to the dietary restrictions that were part and parcel of managing with the condition, some of the 'Specialist' foods that could now help were 2 sugar - free fizzy drinks; 'Tab', a prototype Diet Coke/ pepsi, and, 'Fresco' a fizzy, grapefruit flavoured drink. If I felt like drinking different flavours to Cola or Grapefruit, my fruit squash of taste could be mixed with the flavoured, carbonated water of my choice assisted by the availability, in hardware shops, of pressurized Carbon Dioxide gas cartridges. Therefore, I was able to make my own Orangeade, Limeade and Cherryade. Strangely, I don't recall it being so easy to make my own sugar free Lemonade, but hey! One can't be greedy, I suppose!

So, the Christmas holiday of 1976 came, and went, Thankfully there was less disruption due to my diabetes than there had been in either '74 or '75.

1977.

As 1977 approached, one event, or, more precisely, series of events dominated my mind: It would be my GCE 'O' Level year! An 'O' level was those day's equivalent of the modern day 'GCSE' exam. As such, they were 'make or break' for the majority of school pupils,

There having been no recent '11-Plus' exams held for me or any of my pupil contemporaries in the local 'Comprehensive' schools; owing to the markedly socialist ethos of our local education authority and it's apparent aversion to any policies which emphasised outstanding achievement, and seemed to favour policies emphasising egalitarianism, an 'O' level success was an achievement which did not differ significantly from 11- plus. It simply measured any pupil's academic abilities. It was therefore meant to be a useful measure of that pupil's abilities and provided a measurable, and, I suppose calculable, guidance for their potential employers.

In those days, I would never have regarded myself as particularly academically gifted or inclined, but it's true to say that I never struggled with my schoolwork and I would always prefer learning from textbooks to pursuing the more artisan subjects such as art, woodwork, metalwork or of playing sports, for examples.

In fact, I relished the challenge of the end of year exams and, because 'O' levels were deemed so important, the school had organised a timetabled series of 'Mock' exams to be held at the very beginning of the following spring term; that is to say, the January of 1977.

The exams took place in cold, snowy conditions and, for me, with the dark January days, they imparted a sense of oppressiveness to the opening week and a half of the year.

I did well enough in the exams to persuade the school that I would be a fit person to remain in the 'Grammar' stream of pupils and so I could go on and take the sciences as my chosen subjects at 'O' Level.. In addition to the chosen subjects, there remained the 'Core' subjects of English (study of the language itself AND the literature), Welsh Language and Literature and Maths. So, that would total 8 different subjects to learn and be examined in when the 'O' Levels themselves were held during the following summer term.

Not all my erstwhile classmates did well enough to remain in the grammar stream. The overall result was that the class sizes reduced and the benefit to the school was that the teachers were able to devote more time to individual pupils.

I achieved pass grades in 7 out of the 8 subjects at the end of the academic year. The one paper that I failed was the Welsh Literature exam.

I had kidded myself that that was okay because I never really liked the topic anyway. And so, I felt justified in not putting sufficient effort in over the year and in not prioritising my exam revision.

The 'O' Level exam results would be published in August 1977. My final tally was, that out of my 7 passes, I achieved Grade A in music, Grade B in Maths, English Language and each of the 3 natural sciences, and Grade C in Welsh Language.

But, before the exam results were published, there was, not only. an entire summer of sport to enjoy. Bat also, the BBC had elected to screen an entire summer season of my favourite genre of films/movies namely, 'Horror' films. There would be 2 horror films screened every Friday night over the summer season.

The first film of the week's offering would tend to be a Universal Studios film from, usually, the 1930s and 1940s. So, this included the film with Boris Karloff as Frankenstein's monster, made in 1931. The there was the screening of 'Dracula' starring Bela Lugosi, again filmed in 1931.

I also remember Elsa portrayal of 'Bride of Frankenstein' and I also remember the 'Werewolf' series of films comprising Lon Chaney Jr s performance of 'The Wolfman'.

Not to be outdone, the second film on the weekly double-bill would tend to be a British 'Hammer Horror' film,

The outstanding examples of those Hammer films, made in the second half of the 1950s, throughout the 1960s and the first 5 years of the 1970s were ones that included Christopher Lee, not only in his best known role as 'Count Dracula',filmed in 1958, but also, his performances in the series of Sherlock Holmes movies he made for the studio during the 1950s and early '60s; a 1968 rendition of the novelist Dennis Wheatley's 'The Devil Rides Out' and, as Frankenstein's monster in the film that had first established 'Hammer' as horror film specialists; 'The Curse of Frankenstein', which was released in 1957.

Peter Cushing also co-starred in many of those movies. And, whereas Christopher Lee WAS for many, the definitive Count Dracula, Peter Cushing WAS Baron Frankenstein. He appeared as the driven, but misguided scientist in all but one of the 'Frankenstein' films made and released by Hammer.

The outstanding sports on offer that year included the Australian cricket team's tour of the UK over the summer. They would play a series of 5-day test matches against England spread over the summer from May until the late August bank holiday. But they would also play 1 match against each of the (then 17) first class counties (Durham did not join the first class counties until 1992).

The Australian cricket team had not toured England & Wales since Ian Chappell's team in 1975.

On that occasion, the had been beaten finalists in the inaugural cricket World Cup tournament. Held in England, it featured 50 overs matches held at a variety of grounds that could accommodate Test matches too. The were (in no particular order); Edgbaston, Headingley, Old Trafford, The Oval and Lords. It was the West Indies team that were tournament's winners.

The Australian team of 1975 did not endear themselves to the British public or the British press.

True, that team included many great players, for example, Ian Chappell himself and his brother Greg, Doug Walters, Rodney Marsh (behind the stumps as wicket keeper) and Dennis Lilley who, along with Jeff Thomson, had formed a fearsome pair of fast bowlers when England had toured Australia the previous winter.

I gave included them here because indeed, they came back to tour England in 1977.

That time, there was no Dennis Lilley due to his chronic back injury, but Jeff Thomson DID tour. Greg Chappell also toured, but this time without Ian. There were a handful of new tourists in the squad too, but the sporting press did not seem to rate them quite as highly as they did in 1974 and '75.

Generally too, the weather was not as fine as it had been during the summer of 1975. Having said that, the match against Glamorgan at St Helens' was completed with Australia again winning against the Welsh county.

Overall, the summer of 1977 was quire memorable from a sports spectator perspective. But it was as a listener that I retain my most bittersweet recollections.

It was a year when the British Lions rugby team embarked a long tour of New Zealand. They played a total of 4 test matches against the mighty 'All Blacks' as the national rugby side is termed and, each time the live radio commentary, introduced by Terry Wogan, himself a Rugby fan, from a studio in Broadcasting House, London. As local kick off times were always 3pm on a Saturday afternoon and New Zealand is diametrically opposite the UK on the World's globe, kick off time here would have been 3 A.M. on Friday night/ Saturday morning in the UK.

So, my timetable for the weekends would be; screening of a Universal Studios horror film late on Friday night. Then, screening of a Hammer (or Hammer era) film beginning as soon as the Universal film ended. Finally, listening to live commentary of the New Zealand versus British Isles rugby tests beginning at 3am British Time (BST). As it was school holiday time, and so, I had no classes to attend and as I did not play any sports myself out of school term time, I could stay awake for up to 24 hours on those occasions!

I would be joining my school's lower 6th form in September. This meant that the summer holidays of the year 1977 would be the last time I would see many of my old school-friends before they went into the world of jobs and adult work.

1978.

This would be the year where I would, in mid December, on 11th, attain adulthood.

I remember that, for my birthday, me and my family would accompany me by taking me to the 'Grand Hotel' in Port Talbot for an evening meal.

In those days, as well as being a hotel, the 'Grand' incorporated it's own 'Berni Inn'.

The 'Berni Inns' were a chain of restaurants which were fairly widespread in the British Isles at that time. Established in 1955, the chain expanded to 147 restaurants at their peak. They offered their so - called 'Family Meals' of, typically, a soup - o - the - day followed by steak and chips or Fish and Chips together with a modest side salad, and then topped off with an Ice Cream sundae or 'Cheese & Biscuits' as sweet.

There was the Berni Inn at the Grand Hotel in Port Talbot and so, that is where I celebrated my 18th birthday.

It was at that time, as much as any other that I realised that I didn't have any close friends nearby. I knew plenty of people and was friendly with virtually all from school, but I had no-one I could call up and say'Shall we go out somewhere tonight?, or go to a party, or 'Disco' (theque) on the weekend? Many, but by no means all, of my friends from school had already had they're own 18th birthday parties. In other words, (and not all my schoolfriends had wanted, or had, a party); if their birthdays were celebrated before mine. So all my schoolfriends who had been born in September, October or November of 1960 had already had they're coming of age parties.They were usually held at range of venues local to Swansea including nightclubs in the city, or even as far from my home as the South Gower peninsula.. I would always be invited, but I guess I was just too shy to invite my classmates to my own 18th birthday celebration.

I have always believed that this is much to do with not being schooled locally in Port Talbot, but instead, schooled a significant distance away; up in the Swansea Valley, so far away from my actual home address.

With many of my former friends, familiar faces and colleagues gone, I had now entered the more rarefied atmosphere of the 6th form and 'A' Level studies.

During the later part of 1978, I would also pass my UK driver's test at the first attempt (on 8th October), and get punched on the nose by a fellow A level student at school one day, and, suffer the first ordeals and challenge of severe hypoglycaemic attacks which had arisen because my new diabetic consultant at Port Talbot General Hospital decided to advise use of a new (and 'purer') type of Insulin called 'Leo Retard'.

Leo Retard was claimed to be purer than the older, natural, Beef or Pork derived Insulin products then on the market and which I had been using since I first needed daily Insulin injections on 8th July 1975.

From 1975, through 1976 and 1977 and for at least the first part of 1978, I would have to inject my Insulin using a glass hypodermic syringe. These syringes were a combination of a glass barrel, with a metallic (stainless steel) attachment for the hypodermic needle itself. The needle would have to be exchanged for a new one every day, or at least, no longer than every 2 or 3 days to prevent the pain and discomfort on injection caused by the needle having becoming blunt or dirty.

All this spawned its own ritual. Namely, the sterilising by heat of the injecting equipment.

Every weekend, while I was at home, I would commandeer the kitchen to use its gas hob. There, I would cover the barrel in a clean cotton handkerchief before dropping the used syringe to be sterilised's barrel into a pan of boiling water and leave it to boil for several minutes. This immersion in boiling water would sterilise the syringe and ensure no pathogens or infective debris remained,

Then, I would attach a clean, new, hypodermic needle and so, the syringe would be fit to draw up the required amount of insulin from its vial ready to inject.

With Leo Retard, the need to self - sterilise a syringe was removed when disposable, sterile, plastic syringes were marketed.

They were packed into bags of 10 syringes and so a bag would provide up to perhaps several weeks of daily insulin injections.

So, by 1978, I ought to have been conversant enough with the product to be able use the insulin appropriately, safely and adverse effect free.

That was NOT what happened.

Insulin dosing had, and still is, very much a 'trial and error' exercise but, for some reason, my consultant physician had advised this swap of Insulin preparations accompanied by a 'unit for unit' approach to changing over from the old to the new!

The result was that, virtually every day, I was was getting severe, and longstanding, hypoglycaemic attacks. But this time, there was an added dimension to the shivering, shaky, cold sweats I had been used to.

There was a psychological element too!: During a 'HYPO' after injecting Leo Retard, I always seemed to be inhabiting a surreal, dream - like world where I couldn't think straight. There were also strange visual disturbances where, sometimes, any things, including everyday objects appeared markedly smaller than I knew they actually were. And I had many episodes of shouting, and sometimes they would comprise my vocalising profanities. Not directed at anyone in particular or, as far as I'm aware, containing any particular subject-matter.

The must have been frightening to all around me (in reality, it would be the members of my own family) but when they ended, sometimes forcefully in order to make me consume carbohydrates, I would always feel humble, sheepish or sad.

All symptoms could, in practical reality, be easily and quickly cured by eating or drinking carbohydrate containing foods or drinks. BUT, the most ironic symptom of all was my self- denial that anything was wrong! I still don't know whether this was due to the fact of being 'hypo' itself or, something within my psyche or, maybe even, a mixture of the two, but

I must have put my poor parents and my sister through hell during those attacks. Equally, they would be scary events for any onlooker.

Thankfully, the insulins that are available nowadays seem to be much less psychologically active. They are now all genetically modified products. So, it is impossible to get the same range of adverse effects from accidental and/or unintended overdoses.

THE END OF MY SECONDARY SCHOOLING.

As the summer term approached, I was conscious that not only, would I cease to be a schoolboy shortly, but also, I would be leaving my home, the only house I had lived in for the whole of my life, that I would not see my teachers or school friends again (or at least, very rarely, if ever again).

1979

My interview to be enrolled onto the undergraduate course at the School of Pharmacy, University of London took place over the 1979 summer holiday following the sitting of my exams in the late spring and early summer.

I attended alone and travelled to London Paddington by train, on the then, relatively new 'Inter City 125' trains from Port Talbot station (now, Port Talbot Parkway).

By then, I had enough experience of London to be able to navigate my way, from Paddington station, to the school's premises at 29-39, Brunswick Square, Bloomsbury.

I have already written earlier about the details of how I attended for interview. And what happened at the interview itself.

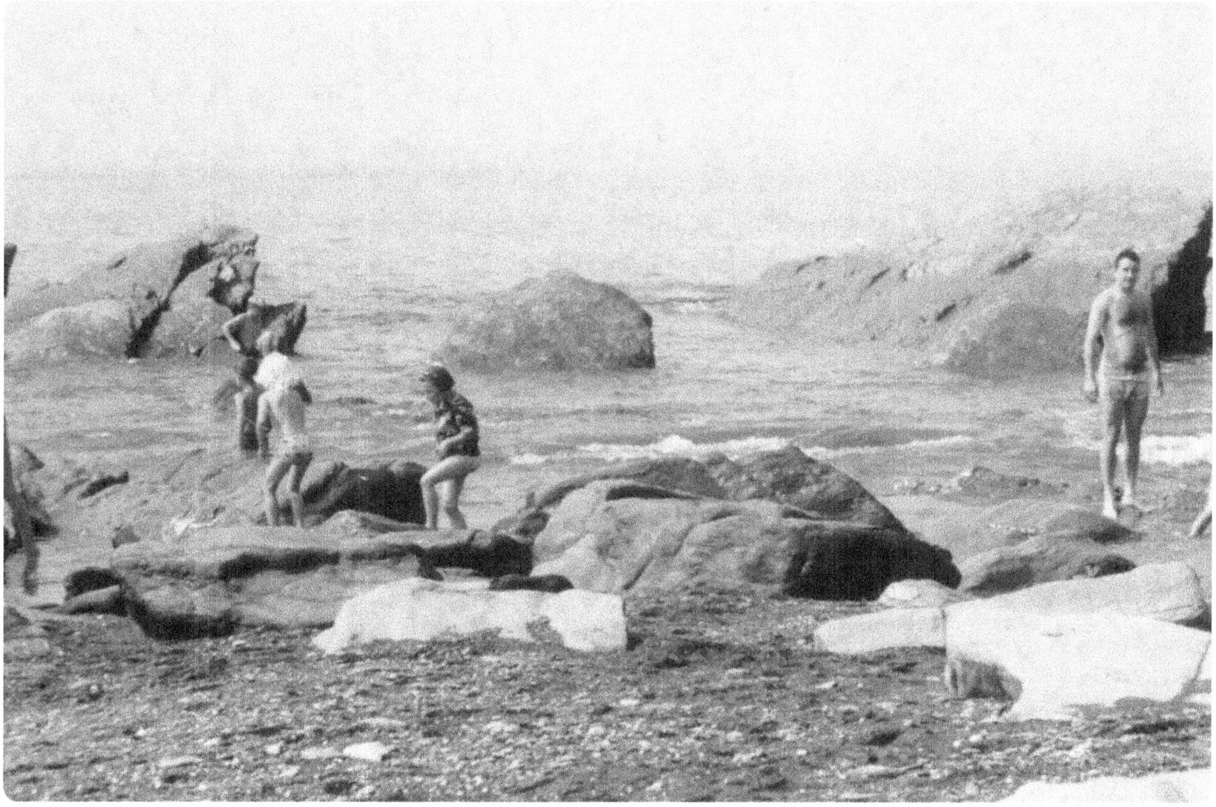

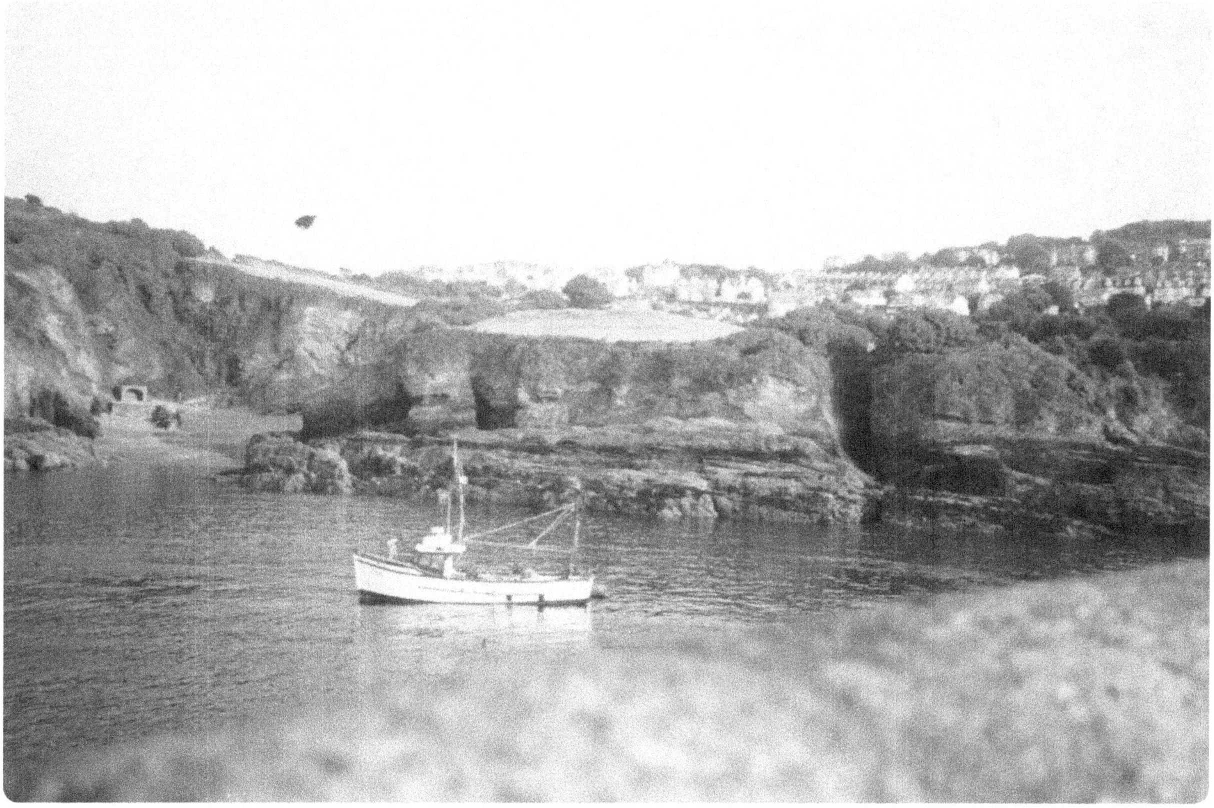

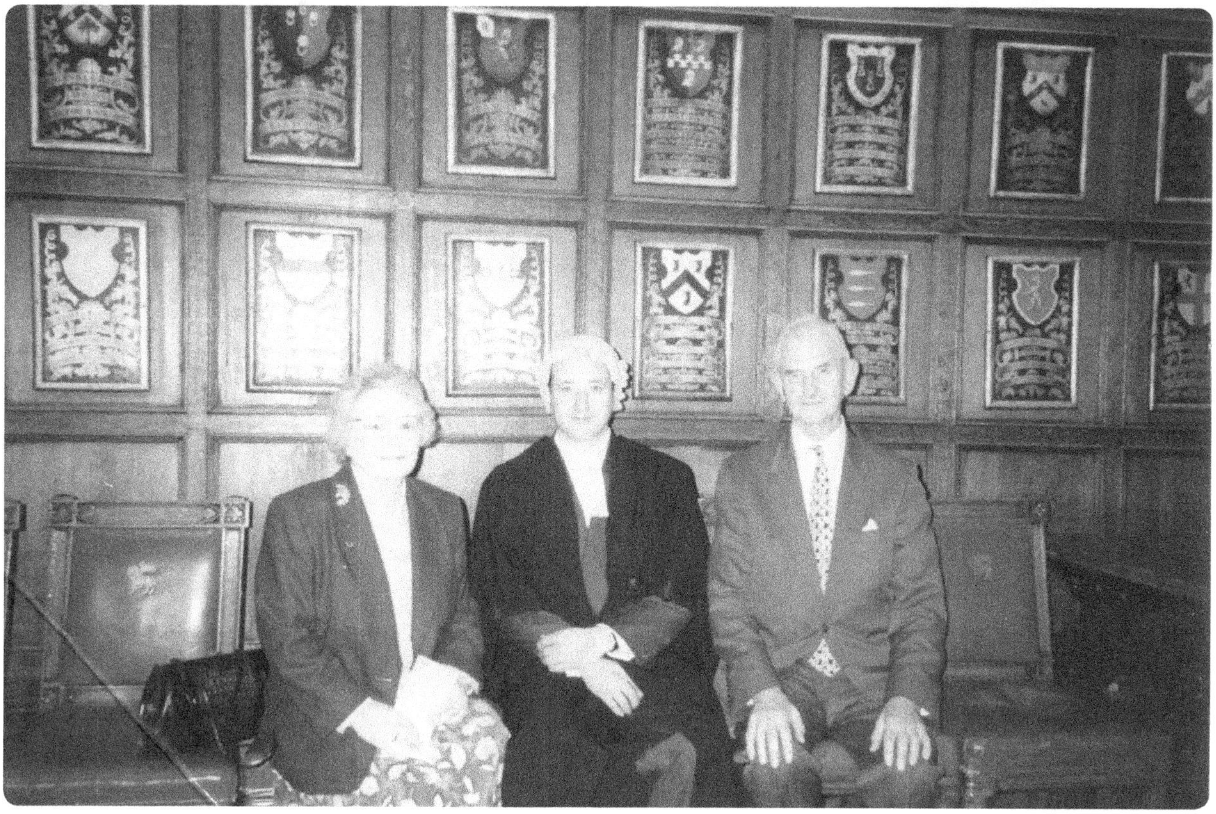

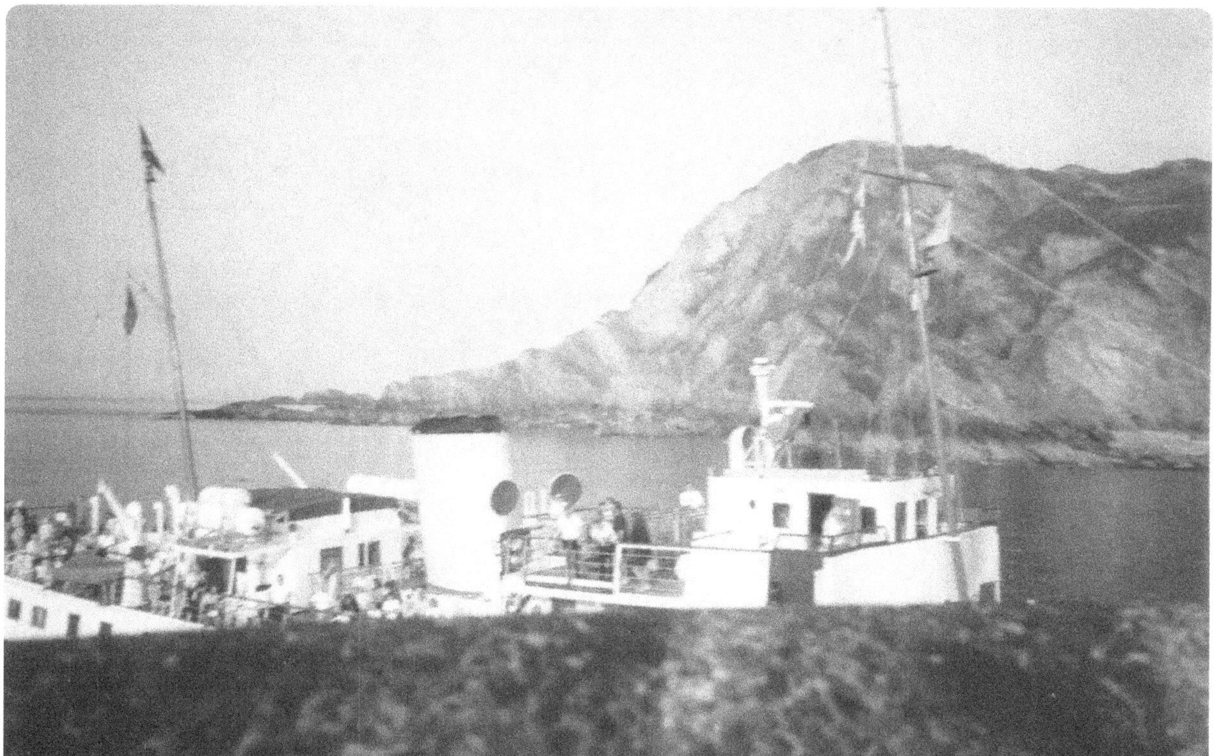

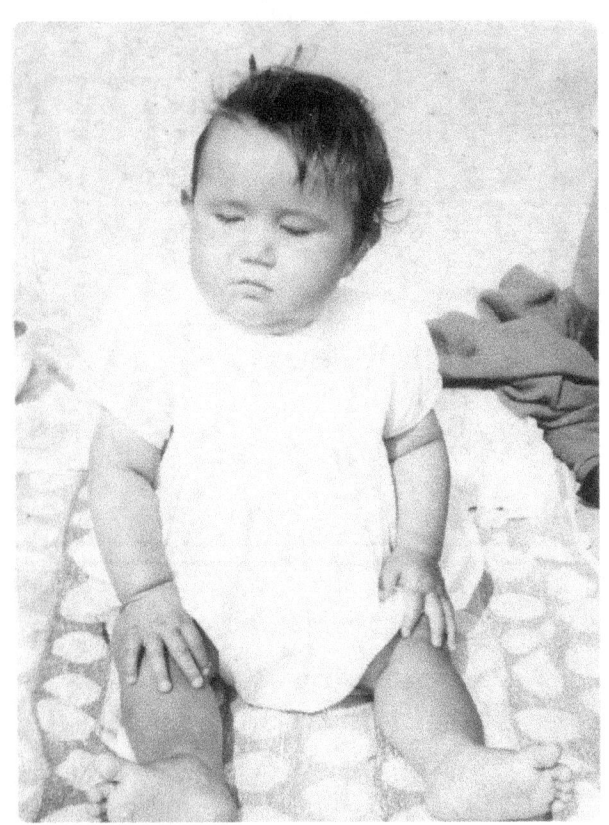

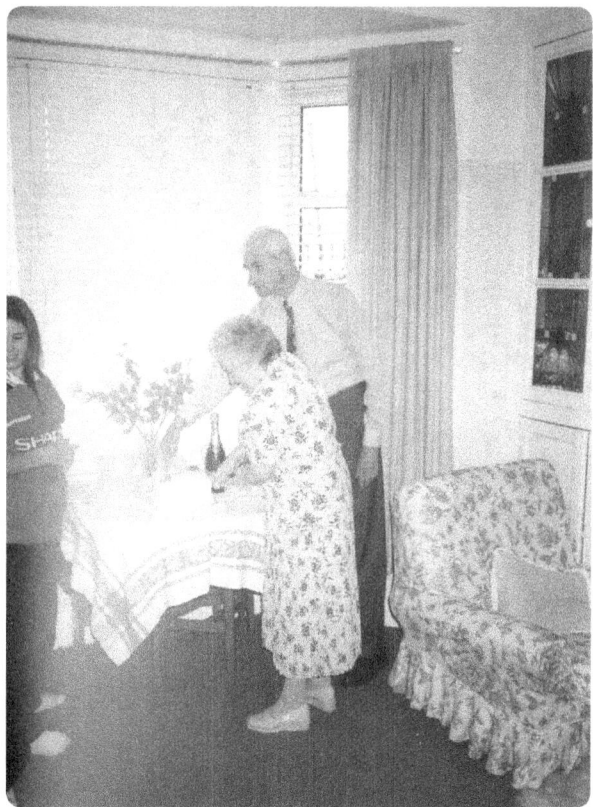

LIFE AS AN UNDERGRADUATE. (1979 -82)

*I*n those days, anyone who wanted to practise as a pharmacist in England, Wales, Scotland or Northern Ireland (including the Channel Isles and Isle of Man) had firstly, to have graduated with a degree in pharmacy and, secondly, had to have satisfactorily completed a pre- registration period of 1 year in a working environment (Community, Hospital or the Pharmaceutical Industry). Only then could they apply for registration. Nowadays, the requirements seem to be even more onerous to any aspiring registrant. All degrees in Pharmacy are now 4 years in length and there is a much more lengthy, and structured, Continuing Professional Development (CPD) requirement for members of the profession.

The necessary skill sets are also different.

When I first worked as a pre-registration graduate and then, as a fully qualified pharmacist, a significant portion of the working day was spent manufacturing the medicines to be issued to patients.

This was termed 'Extemporaneous' dispensing and, I remember having regularly to consult the various 'Pharmacopaeias' for the recipes and methods of preparation for details of the the raw ingredients.

During our student days, regular and, seemingly un-ending assessments were undertaken and our finished products constantly checked for, not only fitness for use, but also safety, compliance with legal and regulatory requirements as well as appropriate, and accurate, record keeping.

There were tutorials where we students would break in to small groups of no more than a dozen. Often, this would be to take a very esoteric topic and examine it closely; even perhaps with post - graduates and members of teaching staff involved.

There were also lectures given to the entire year's student body.

Mondays, Tuesdays, Thursdays and Fridays always began with 2 separate lectures covering one of the 5 core disciplines. These core disciplines were, in no specific order, a) Chemistry (of pharmaceuticals), b) Microbiology affecting pharmaceuticals. So, for instance, we would learn to appreciate the factors that led to the bacterial spoilage of drug products, c) the subject of 'Pharmaceutics' which encompassed the principles of drug formulation, d) Pharmacology (which was the study of how and why various drugs acted on the body in different ways and e) pharmacognosy, which focused on what drugs were actually made FROM. Some drugs originate from plants e.g. Digitalis which strengthens the heart. Some drugs are derived from animal sources for example, the early formulation of commercially available Insulins. Yet others are entirely synthetic, but made to mimic (or oppose) the action of substances naturally present in the body e.g. Adrenaline or Steroids or Hormones.

Wednesdays were our semi-free day. Organised sports were alway arranged for the afternoons. The school had Soccer, Rugby Union and Cricket teams were already established in existence at all levels of proficiency and the competition among students for places in these teams could sometimes be quite intense! This was also the time for lectures; but often on lighter subjects than the above core subjects,

There were also practical classes galore!

These were held every weekday afternoon EXCEPT, of course, Wednesdays due to the sports programs on offer.

After our two, daily, hour - long lectures, held in the so - called 'Large Lecture theatre, we students would be entitled to a short, 15 minute break, before trooping to the upper floors for our practical sessions.

The school building was constructed using a basement, then 5 upper floors. In fact, there was actually, a 6th floor too. This was empty during my first 2 years, but in my 3rd year, a separate, 'Toxicology' department began offering its own 3 year degree course with it's own intake of students. It may well have been as much a question of lack of time, opportunities, or some other reason; but we did not seem to mix socially with any of the Toxicology staff or students. I wonder if any of them went onto make names for themselves in this field?

The building's basement area was used for the students' personal property. Each student were given they're own locker and were also given a unique key so that only they could access it and lock too it when it was not in use. Most of us stored our overcoats, bags, plastic ring - binder files for the day and anything else not needed for our day's classes.

The ground floor was reserved for the school's administration, It included the Dean's office. It was also where any visitors to the school would have to undergo I.D. procedures and leave when they're business was over.

The ground floor also incorporated the 'Refectory' where our lunches and refreshments could be bought.

The school also retained its own resident chef - a man with an absolutely huge and loud laugh!

One knew that all was well with the world if you heard chef booming 'HA HA HA HAH HA' at any point during the day!

The menus were basic, but when I and most of my co-students were living off our local authority grants, and so, had limited budgets, here was very little call for expensive foods.

As students, the refectory's freshly cooked chips and beef burgers provided sufficient sustenance, sometimes for the whole day.

The chips were 'self - service' and were obtained by dipping a ladle into a huge vat of fried tubers.

I suppose the catering staff had they're own restrictions on portion size, but often, the strident, eyeball to eyeball accusation of; 'YOU GOT TOO MUCH CHIPS' was bellowed at some unfortunate, and hungry, student!

Naturally, no admissions are made in relation to whether your author was ever unfortunate, or greedy at lunchtimes in the School's refectory......!

What I DID get involved with, was participation among the various organised groups that the Student's Union provided for us. There was a chess club,a music club for the pianists among us, and societies for Indian students, and other South East Asians such as Singaporean, Taiwanese or Hong Kong students. a Christian Union. I, of course, belonged to the Rugby Club. I was a keen player. I belonged to the Rugby club. I achieved a place, not only in The School of Pharmacy's team, but also, in a combined School of Pharmacy/Royal Free Hospital rugby team 'SOP/RFH'. This ensured that, on every day I was free from studies or, from practical classes, I was representing my college, as SOP/RFH' player on one of the many sports grounds in London and the surrounding areas.

On these occasions, the school's soccer, hockey, netball or, in summer, the cricket team would be playing. Our 'home' sports pitches were situated at 'Myddleton House' in Enfield, Middlesex. This was many miles away from the school's buildings and laboratories of Bloomsbury, in central

London as, of course, there would have been insufficient space there to accommodate multiple sports pitches, changing areas, car parks and associated structures.

So, we would assemble as a team at the school at lunchtime on sports days, then we would have to travel the 10 plus miles to our grounds at Myddleton House (named after the 17th century Welsh - born benefactor, Sir Hugh Myddleton - (a pioneer of clean water for the mass population) by chartered coach and play our match, Then, no doubt, we would enjoy some drinks afterwards and finally, we would travel back to London and our individual lodgings or houses afterwards.

I enjoyed my time as an undergraduate at the school immensely. In addition to my sporting exploits on the rugby field every Wednesday and Saturday afternoon, there was always a 'Disco.' held in the junior common room on Friday nights where we could let off steam with fellow students and which became a regular feature of undergraduate student life. Romance was always a feature of our student interactions and countless romantic relationships were often made and broken in quick succession. Quite a few relationships did prevail, and at least 2 pairings from we, of the 1979 - 82 intake remain as happily marrieds even to this day.

Personally, I did not settle into a long - term relationship with anyone from the college but happily, there are still yearly re - unions held of which I have been invited to attend and have done so, and have always been left with happy memories.

The research being carried out at the time and the academic records and histories of the staff and post graduates from the school was always very impressive, and had been since the school was first incepted, well over a century earlier, in 1842.

Many decades later, and well after I had left, after graduation, the so-called 'Salisbury poisonings' made headline news worldwide when it appeared that a nerve agent was being used to murder some of the enemies, or suspected enemies, of the Russian state. The nerve agent's properties included some signs and symptoms of chemical compounds that reminded me of one of the classes of chemicals that were included among the subjects of my studies at the school of pharmacy. This was principally because I remembered that, among the prominent signs and symptoms of anti-cholinesterase poisoning are; firstly, paralysis of respiratory muscles particularly the 'skeletal' muscles that are found in the body's diaphragm and are responsible for being able to breathe in, and out. Secondly, loss of consciousness and eventual death and, thirdly, that the chemicals are able to enter the body in the first place, by being absorbed through contact with the skin.

The short, reported name of the implicated chemical was 'Novichok'. The details of the news reports that were broadcast on TV, radio, and the newspapers, reminded me of the actions of 'Anti - cholinesterases', a class of chemical compound that was well known to me, and to anyone else, who have either studied or worked at The School of Pharmacy.

The specialist tests done, the time, from the Porton Down centre, on behalf of the British government, confirmed that 'Novichok' was, in fact, an 'Anti - Cholinesterase type agent. It was easily absorbed into the 'tissues, difficult to detect, toxic in very small amounts and, of course, almost invariably, lethal!

Acetylcholine is a natural chemical, necessary for life, and is an ubiquitous 'neuro- transmitter' found in the human (and all other animal's) bodies. The term 'Neuro - transmitter' means that it a chemical entity that is secreted by glands in the body, has an action at the junction of nerve tissue and the nerve's associated muscles and therefore is responsible, in the animal, or human being's ability to breathe, move and contract muscles using the body's musculature.

There are essentially 3 different types of 'muscle' namely, Cardiac muscle, which, as its name implies, is found only in the heart, 'smooth' muscle, which is found lining the intestines and inside major blood vessels e.g. veins and arteries and, 'skeletal' muscle which is responsible for our ability walk, run and move around or of course, to STOP walking, running or moving around, at will.

It is readily destroyed by the body too, and its waste products will then either be excreted by the body or, recycled in our Livers and Kidneys. The class of chemicals that destroy it in our bodies are the enzymes known as the 'Cholinesterases'

Therefore, an ANTI - Cholinesterase has the property of never allowing the victim's nervous system to 'switch off', to pause, or work properly again whether under our will's control or whether automatically e.g. as in a 'Reflex' reaction.

That is why 'Novichok' is so dangerous a chemical.

Unfortunately, this knowledge came known publicly and to the authorities, when it was too late to save the lives of many of its victims, some of whom were entirely innocent of any crimes or any malfeasance against the Russian state, But, at least we, in the free and civilised countries, knew what we were up against!

Of course, I cannot claim any personal involvement in any of the school's work since I left in 1982. Nor, of course, can I claim anything other than a passing interest in reading about their work in the media, or about the achievements of other independent individuals, agencies or institutions.

But, I will always have my degree certificate and the associated memories of my time at the school.

After graduation, one had to get a job.

1982/83

The first thing I recall around these days, was the opportunity to go to Innsbruck, Australia on a ski- ing trip.

S. o P. student's union had organised this week long excursion complete with ski slope passes and hire of ski-ing equipment at reasonable rates.

I booked myself on to the trip, even though the prospect of spending the days getting up a slippery, slidey mountainside (The Axamer Lizum) before then descending the very same route with a pair of waxed sticks under my feet, did not fill me with any sense of adventure or fun, so I elected instead, to walk as much as I could during the day and then re-join my fellow student skiers for the evening's mainly alcohol fuelled, evenings.

Innsbruck itself was a moderate sized town in the Austrian Bavarian Alps. It had just finished a stint as the host city for the 1982 Winter Olympic Games and so, all the necessary equipment and downhill ski venues were within easy reach.

For example, it was possible to walk to the top of the Ski-Jump slide and look at the view! There was a rather 'tongue in cheek' account of how the view from the top of the course looked directly in to a cemetary in one's direct eye line as would be seen by anyone prepared to actually use the ski jump slope!

Having taken the opportunity to get my own view from the top of the slope, I certainly admired the ski jumper's braveness!

So, during our final ever term as students at the school (spring/summer term 1982), the major pharmaceutical employers; the industry e.g. the firms of Smith, Kline, and French (SKF), Glaxo (now part of Glaxo/SmithKline), Fisons,(of weed killer notoriety), Merch, Sharpe and Dohme (MSD) and many other multi national members of 'Big Pharm' attended at our school to see if our talent was the type of human resource they were looking for. The answer, in many cases, was 'Yes' and many of my fellow students have ended up working for the pharmaceutical industry.

There was also the Hospital sector (either for NHS or private hospitals - although both were represented).

If one didn't fancy joining, or were not selected to join those career paths, I, like the majority of other students joined the 'Community' Pharmacy sector. In short, I would be applying for a job in a 'Chemist's Shop'

Part of the mainly corporate gravy train that attended the 'Square' on that day to look for, and fish for, the new graduate talent were; deputations from 'Boots the Chemist's head office in Nottingham. There was also a contingent from 'Underwoods' chemists; a large multiple chemist business with perhaps a hundred, or so outlets, mainly in London and the Southeast of England, Also present, (from my memory) were representatives of 'Lloyd's Chemist'. That firm would quickly grow to be the biggest independent competitor to the mighty 'Boots organisation', and to do so within only a few, short years.

The community pharmacy sector was beginning to boom, fostered by a more business oriented political ethos at the time. The Conservative Party had come to power at the May 1979 General Election and so, by mid 1982, Mrs Margaret Thatcher was firmly ensconced at 10, Downing Street as Prime Minister - position she was to hold for over a decade, only finally ceding power in 1990.

I remember the sense of sheer competition between all of us, as new graduates. Even though we were still all friends and colleagues, we were about to enter the competitive world of working in a learned profession and with the purpose of serving members of the public we encountered. In other words, our 'Communities'.

But, in amongst the 'hubbub', I had noticed a small, written advertisement at the jobs' fair.

PRE - REG.
PHARMACIST TIMES

*I*t was from an independent chemist in Canning Town, London E16 and invited applications for graduate training positions as 'Pre- Registration Trainees' or, colloquially, referred to as 'pre-Reg's'.

That evening, I called the number.

I introduced myself and told the person on the other end what the purpose of my call was. The male voice on the other end of the line asked me a little about myself. Name, age, and what school of pharmacy I had been attending and whether I had successfully graduated and, if so, what class of degree I had been awarded. He seemed very nervous and, to be frank, so was I. He asked me to visit the shop during its opening hours, but to do so early in the working day, since it was, he claimed, a very busy shop.

He gave me the address; it was in a street called 'Hermit Road', at number 21, in a place I'd never previously heard of; Canning Town, London E16.

I checked on how to get to Canning Town by using a combination of the London A to Z street maps, checking the tube lines diagram, checking Underground timetables or British Rail route maps. That exercise was not so straightforward in 1982 as it would be today. I found that, in those days there, WAS a British Rail station at Canning Town which, according to the A to Z was within easy walking distance by turning left off the main London to southern Essex road (the A13) at Hermit Road itself. But, the exact timetable was difficult to consult without physically going to the station itself, the trains were, being from the older rolling-stock models, quite uncomfortable to travel on.

Nowadays, the situation is entirely different: Canning Town has its own tube station on the 'Jubilee' line (in addition to also being on the old, British Railways tracks)and, is also served by many London Bus routes from a transport 'Hub'- like station building which has an attached shopping mall! It has excellent, integrated diagrammed, easily accessible, timetables and electronic (dot - matrix) train destination indicators which are constantly updating so the you can tell, not only, which direction the the next train is headed, but also, how long you will have to wait before it arrives/departs. Information is also updated as to any delays en - route.

But, on that 1982 day, had put my smart clothes on with clean shirt, sweater, shoes and made sure my hair was neat and tidy.

I was to meet the shop's proprietor and its Pharmacy's manager, a Mr Patel and A*****, respectively.

I saw that the shop itself was in part of a small parade. It was right next door to a Doctors' surgery and there were signs of a constant traffic of members of the public of all physical descriptions going to, or from, mainly, the Chemist's shop.

Gingerly, I pushed the front door open.

Facing me, at the shop's 'counter' area, were 2 youngish looking ladies. Both were dressed in their ordinary day clothes. One, an Asian - looking girl was wearing a bright and ornately looking outfit incorporating a sari, she had long, dark, hair. The other, had white skin, short, ginger coloured hair. and was wearing ordinary jeans. Both had an identical, patterned, design, of shop overall.

We all looked at each other briefly. But none of us said a word!

Suddenly, there came rather ostentation sounding shriek from the back of the shop area; 'Oooh!. I think he's here' exclaimed the female voice's owner. 'Hello - o- o'!

Almost immediately, a much older woman with shortish (but seemingly, heavily dyed), hair, lashings of facial make - up, and a heavy plastering of dark, red lipstick appeared, smiling ' than the 2 girls at the shop's counter looking.

'Hello. I'm Adele' she said, smiling.

Behind her, a middle aged Asian looking gentleman almost, peeped from behind her. He gave no verbal introduction, but held out his hand to offer a rather limp, and perfunctory, handshake. It was Mr Patel, the shop's owner and proprietor.

We had a fairly lengthy, and quite profound interview. I was asked about myself and also, I was given the chance to ask questions to them myself.

Throughout, there was a constant flow of patients and customers coming in to the shop. It certainly WAS busy. Far busier than the previous times I had assisted at pharmacies while I was an undergraduate student.

Although I had already done an unqualified 'Medicines Counter' assistant's job when I was a Pharmacy student at Boots the Chemist's shop in Bridgend, Mid Glamorgan over the summer of 1980. This was directly after I had finished, and passed the first my of my 3 years of degree studies. I had followed that up with a summer's work at Neath General Hospital over the school's summer break in 1981, I had never before been properly paid other than out of pocket expense rates for my time.

LIFE IN EAST LONDON.

ow. I would be on a salary! A 'Pre- Reg's' salary. Pre Reg salary's rates were fixed by the Pharmaceutical Society of Great Britain (then known as the 'PSGB' for short). It would work out at about 1/3rd of the rate that a fully qualified pharmacist manager of the time, would get. So, it wasn't brilliant money, but it would suffice to pay my rent, for food, for leisure and, importantly at that stage of my career, there was a modest surplus at the end of each pay period. This would be saved or partially spent on my annual holiday entitlement.

During the whole of that year (late 1982 into the first part of 1983), I lived in a shared house in Leyton, London E10. I lived with several other people, who came, and went on short-term lets and who seemed to keep themselves very much to themselves. Occasionally, there would be parties. I didn't stay in touch with anyone from that time and remember precious little about any of the encounters I had; save for one: At one of those parties, a very beautiful young lady guest came up to me and we soon got talking. She told me she was a 'Russian Spy'! I didn't know whether she was joking or not. The 'Cold War' between East and West was still very much going at the time and naturally, I wouldn't have wanted any trouble. In the end, we both became the proverbial 'Ships that pass in the night' but, it was a charming few hours we spent in each other's company.

The house was in a road called Warren Road in E10. It was owned, apparently, by a 'Mr Meisels'. He was not living there himself and the whole place seemed damp. There was absolutely no heating for any of the rooms, including my room (a modified bedroom or 'bed-sit'). If I wanted warmth I would have to deploy my small, 2 - bar, electric fire at my own cost. All electrical connections for the house had their own, discreet connection to the mains' supply. So each occupant of a 'bed sit' would have their own electricity account and were billed seperately to all other bed-sits. All in all, it was hardly a comfortable existence! But, at least I had the consolation of being on decent pay.

Imagine my amusement, when, a few years later, long after I had left the house, a current-affairs documentary was broadcast on one of the mainstream TV channels (so either BBC or ITV, or, possibly, Channel 4 which had begun broadcasting for the 1st time in late 1983, broadcast a programme alleging that Mr Meisels was in fact, a rogue landlord. This was not that long after the scandal involving Gerald Ratner; a rogue landlord who was violent toward his tenants, or erstwhile tenants, if they ever got behind with their rental payments!

To set my record straight; I personally, never encountered any trouble with Mr Meisels other than there was no heating anywhere in the house AND that the winter of 1982-83 was VERY cold!

Leyton it self was a decent enough place. It is roughly equidistant between Hackney to the South, Walthamstow, to it's west and Ilford and Wanstead, to it's east.

There were marvellous transport connections to each of those destinations. This made it easy to enjoy, and participate in many local amenities.

I remember becoming a member at 'Wanstead Leisure Centre' where payment of a monthly fee entitled members to weight training, circuit training or gym work. To cap it all, there was a large social circle where arrangements for meals out at local restaurants, dances, quizzes and the like were in place.

I was kind of glad that I was a single person, as it meant I did not have to get a partner's agreement to be able to attend any event.

Wanstead, London E11 was also the location for monthly local Pharmaceutical Society 'branch' meetings (the 'East Metropolitan; Branch), where a range of lecturers, talks, films, exhibitions of art or photography and the like were organised for registered pharmacists, students and pre-registration graduates, like myself.

In addition, there was always a sumptuous buffet available or, very occasionally, a 3 course meal in the restaurant attached to the venue.

For the latter, one had to be invited, or be one of the branch's committee members.

In the early years, following my registration as a pharmacist, I became interested in the general work of the RPSGB at its 'Branch' level and within a few years, I was myself approved on to the committee.

I particularly remember the year 1985 when I was appointed a branch representative to RPSGB's Annual General Meeting and where I attended the all-day event at the RPSGB's headquarters, then situated in Lambeth, central London.

On the day, I joined 3 of my branch colleagues as representatives of the 'East Met.' branch and we each made our own way to the meeting, stayed, and voted as delegates of the branch or spoke on relevant topics or participated in the policy-forming debates which inevitably preceded each vote.

The venue for each of these monthly meetings was at Wanstead Public Library which was in the marvellously named 'Spratt Hall Road' E11.

The monthly meetings were generally well attended with perhaps around 50 or more delegates at the most popular meetings, for example, where a well known guest speaker or a major personality from the Pharmaceutical had been booked. Only scarcely, were there less than 30 for the less fortunate occasions where, perhaps, there were also weather or transport difficulties.

Aside from Wanstead Library, for hosting its programme of monthly pharmacy branch meetings, the Wanstead leisure centre for my weekend keep- fit endeavours and for easy transport links to Central London via the Hainault branch of the central line tube, my ambitions lay in, eventually, being able to buy my own house.

Therefore, I was gradually getting readier to move on from my life in and around NorthEast London.

I decided to look for somewhere that, geographically, was fairly close to the Leyton area, but had a better standard of housing stock yet, still being within my budget.

I still did not feel ready for a mortgage, with it's 'baggage' of permanence in financial outgoings, associated insurance policies, associated life insurance policies, risks and, the fact that, age wise, I was still in my mid 20s and had no realistic prospects of settling down to marriage very soon. I decided to look for an affordable rental property in South Woodford, London E18 as a place to live in and work from (pro tem)..

I knew several people who lived in the area and that I trusted. I consulted local newspapers and visited quite a number of letting/sales agents too.

Eventually, I came across a large house for rent in a fairly quiet and secluded street.

I applied, and was introduced to family that would share my abode for the next couple of years. They lived in a large house on top of a hill and had several bedrooms available to lodgers. All the other guests were working, and all were single, male people. The only woman was the house proprietor's rather attractive partner

I settled in, decided that I liked the area, as well as the house, its occupants and its living arrangements. But I had the feeling, and the hope, that this was NOT going to be the area, place or house that I would be spending the rest of my life in!

By now, we were well in to the mid 1980s. But the bank's borrowing interest rates had still not peaked, it was obvious that the whole British economy was booming, This was the era of comedian Harry Enfield's 'Loadso'money' character and Mrs Thatcher's economic policies seemed to be working. Industrial depression, striking coal miners and family deprivation seemed a million miles away from my settled existence at the time, living, and working in one of the world's major, and most wealthy, cities. Surely, NOW was the time to get myself on my feet and settle down.

MY DALLIANCE AS A CHEMIST SHOP'S PROPRIETOR. (1986– 88)

*O*newish chemist's shop came on to the market very close to where I was living. It already had the ability to allow it to dispense NHS and private doctor's prescriptions, seemed as if it was well situated on a High Road in a wealthy area and even had two upper floors which could form the basis for upgrading to rental property.

It seemed perfect.

I made enquiries with the property's estate agents.

It was still available, but, I was advised to move quickly, before its asking price increased too much and took it away from my affordability.

As a pharmacy, the shop's estate agents specialised in handling the sale and purchase of that type of premises, so I set about finding a decent firm of solicitors who I could instruct to handle my purchase.

I found a firm in a nearby town; Stratford, London E15. Of course, that location would later be chosen as the venue for the 2012 Olympic Games and the whole area has by now been transformed from the Stratford, London E15 that I remember from the earlier part of the 1980s.

It is now a modern, up to date, clean, desirable and wealthy area which bears little comparison to the Stratford of 1983 which, by comparison was a run down conglomeration of ugly high rise blocks (for example, the infamous 'Henniker Point'), multiple railway sidings which, at the time, were popularly alleged to be used for transporting nuclear waste and other toxic materials, and various run-down shopping parades, shops and rough pubs.

SOUTH WOODFORD

I complied with the necessary legal formalities, contracts were exchanged with the vendor and a finance company called 'Statim' Finance agreed to fund the balance of the shop's purchase price over the amount that I was able to finance myself from my savings.

The big mistake that I made was that I was overstretching myself because, I ended up borrowing just under 80% of the total price.

The chemist shop that I ran was situated in the North eastern corner of London, in an area called South Woodford.

It was a fairly wealthy area, even allowing for the relative wealth of London and the South East when compared with most other regions of the UK.

Many of my customers fell in to 2 main brackets: The wealthy, retirees and the Young, upwardly mobile, professional classes, or the much younger folk, with young families and children (or the 'YUPPIES' as they became colloquially referred to).

Examination of the shop vendor's accounts and trade invoices for the past periods of trade were revealed to me, both by right and by custom as part of the shop vending papers.

They were useful in planning for the type, and amount, of stock I would need to be able to run a successful (and lucrative) concern.

In addition to the drugs and pharmaceutical preparations, there would also be 'OTCs', that is, medicines which the public could by without a doctor's prescription, toiletries, perfumes, sanitary products and anything else that was customarily sold in pharmacies. Examples were Aspirin tablets, Paracetamol tablets, various proprietary cough and cold mixtures, Aqueous cream BP (for maintaining soft skin on the hands), Emulsifying Ointment BP (for mollifying hard skin), Simple

Linctus (for symptomatic relief of coughs and colds), corn plasters and other sundry remedies. Finally, there were the 'odds and sods' - things that had traditionally been sold in the local area, namely, North East London.

I had noticed a large demand for disposable, branded baby's nappies with corresponding volumes of sales.

It appeared that my shop's vendor had cut the prices of these in an attempt, no doubt, to attract customers in to the shop.

The problems with that approach were that firstly, the shop's overall margin profitability tended to be reduced. Secondly, the outer nappy packs were very bulky, thus reducing the amount of shop space for the stocking of other,no less profitable, goods.

The trends were no better than reasonable at any time. I worked long opening hours (9am to 7pm on weekdays, 9 to 5.30pm on Saturdays. Then, a day off on Sunday for leisure activities...... except, more and more, I would find myself going to the Wholesaler's (some 6 or 7 miles away) to re-stock or perhaps fill some special order for an unusual product that had been asked for by a customer during the week.

On the whole, it was a sufficiently profitable business; there was the regular, and safe, income from the fees for dispensing NHS prescriptions, the more profitable private Doctors' prescriptions, over -the - counter (OTC) medicine sales and all manner of other goods that were customarily sold from Chemist shops. Until, that is, one looked at the sheer amount of time that had to be devoted to the shop's upkeep.

Two doors down from my shop, I had noticed a rather attractive girl who sometimes came in to my shop. Many of the other staff members visited too on their staff breaks et cetera and, of course, we all got talking:

I learnt that her name was Maria.

I gathered that she was fairly recently married, but that there were no children.

One day, when she same in to my shop on her tea break, I discovered that her husband was, apparently, cheating on her. They were both living at the time in their first house as owners/ occupiers. It was nearby, in Woodford Green. Would I be present for the next occasion where inteamaritaln trouble and/or strife was anticipated?

I must confess, I was rather taken aback by her suggestion!

I was not, after all, a marriage counsellor or a social worker!

But, as we were both friendly towards each other, spoke every day, and were almost work colleagues; what with her also working long hours, just 2 doors away from my shop, and, that she had, by know told me that her marriage was over and that divorce had been filed for, I agreed.

We began to see a lot more of each other outside work and, one day, she invited me to meet her parents who, at the time, were working, and living, in a nearby town in central Essex.

I did not have a wife, partner or girlfriend at the time. So, I agreed.

It must have been obvious by that stage, that me and Maria were an item!

We would stay overnight together (usually at Maria's parents' house, (occasionally in the spare bedroom at her sister's house) and, of course, nature soon took its course.

Maria fell pregnant!

On Easter Monday, 4th April 1988, my (now, sadly, late and much missed) daughter was born at Whipps Cross hospital in Leytonstone, London E11. This was the NHS unit that served our area. I still remember many details about the birth. Firstly, I was allowed to be present at the birth!vThis was by no means automatic for new fathers at that time. But, as I was a practising pharmacist, the hospital authorities and the staff on the maternity ward were prepared to allow me to stay and be present to witness my first child's birth; the obstetrician was an unbelievably tall, and thin, Irishman with a rather ironic sounding surname! I shall not repeat his name here for fear of causing embarrassment.

But of course, I was delighted!

We called her 'Sian' which is the Welsh language version of Jane.

All of my spare time was now being spent in Sian and Maria;s presence, whether we were alone, or, as often happened, were with my in - laws and often, with their friends, families and associates too.

It was a a very social, and happy, time.

Back in the 'real' world of day to day working life; Although bank interest rates were still low at the time, I had not been allowed to arrange for sufficient leeway to cope with any future increases in those rates. And, in the events that transpired, the shop itself really wasn't busy enough to justify such a big percentage loan that I had incurred on it..

Although I was holding an NHS contract to dispense my prescriptions, I did not have sufficient private work, or non-prescription sales (eg Perfumes, Make - Up, confectionery and the like) to support myself if the economic climate changed for the worse.

Unfortunately. It did!

The financial 'Bubble' of the mid 1980s finally, and well and truly, burst!

Very quickly, the UKs chancellor of the exchequer (then Nigel Lawson), was forced to increase the bank's interest rates to 15% from their previous, mid - single figure, levels.

This proved crippling, not just to me, but for many of the other budding entrepreneurs of the time.

It was NOT a good time to borrow money from the banks, and, in my naivety, I, and many others, fell victim.

I put the shop back up for sale, and, fortunately, I was able to find a buyer from among the advertisements I put in the trade press under "Shop for Sale"!

The overall experience was a little hair-raising, if not, downright unpleasant at times, but I still maintain that it stood me in good stead.

But, on 8th July 1988, I married Maria!

I would now joint a 'Pharmacist Locum' agency.

I, in fact, joined 2 separate agencies, one quite local to me in London, and the other, which had a wider, national coverage of work.

Together, they found me plenty of 'Locum' work over many years.

The word 'Locum' is the Latin word for 'Traveller, and, that exactly described what I did.'

I had, and enjoyed well over 15 years of satisfying, lucrative and, sometimes challenging work. I would normally obtain my bookings over the telephone, or by word of mouth. Then, at the appointed time, I would make the journey to the hospital or shop, that required my services.

Sometimes, it would be just for a single day, to cover one of the regular staff's days off, or emergency sickness, the regular staff member wanting to attend they're own appointments e.g. a dentist or doctor's appointments.

I preferred longer stints, particularly if the shop or hospital was a long way from my home or harder to get there in my car or some similar reason.

Often too, it would be for a longer term booking to cover events like the shop proprietor's annual holiday, or they're long term sickness. Although, thankfully, such occasions were comparatively rare.

Among my notable and most memorable week-long bookings were in; Ilfracombe, Ipswich Nuffield Hospital (a private hospital), Tenby, Newbury, and my vast majority of bookings, which were from London and the South East. There was absolutely nowhere I wouldn't go! 'Have certificate, will travel!' became my motto. There are many more destinations that I simply cannot now remember due to sheer passage of time.

I did shops that had just a single proprietor, larger shops with their own team of regular staff and also 'Multiple' Chemists such as Boots, Superdrug, Sainsbury's or Tesco.

The chemist shops (with just one notable, multiple - shop exception) were always very good at paying my invoices.

An added bonus was, that if I did a stint particularly well, word of mouth, or the 'Bush Telegraph' would operate so that I would also get recommendations from places that I'd not previously worked at.

I did not allow my workload to become so onerous that I would be having to turn down offers.

The only places I did not work in were Scotland (on the grounds that it would have been too far to travel) or Northern Ireland or the Isle of Man): too impractical to go from my London or Essex base.

Over my entire career as a pharmacist, between 1983 and 2005, I am grateful to 2 seperate Locum agencies for keeping me well provided for.

They were; Firstly, in both alphabetical and chronological order, 'Capital Locums', (then based in Chigwell, Essex; but have since moved to Buckhurst Hill/Loughton), and, 'Provincial Pharmacy Locum Services' (PPLS), based in Birmingham.

So, by keeping myself busy, I made a very good living.

During the financial boom years of the mid to late 1980s,

TAWE PHARMACY

As my career proceeded, I felt I was doing enough to justify my practising status notwithstanding that I, as members, had to pay my annual retention fee to the Royal Pharmaceutical Society.

There were branch, regional and Nationally organised means of keeping up to date with relevant developments. Collectively referred to by the abbreviation 'CPD', this was entirely voluntary from as far back as the early 1980s. Now, it has become a mandatory requirement for all pharmacists in whichever field of practice they work, to hold a valid practising certificate. A further requirement for practising as a pharmacist is that one must be registered with The General Pharmaceutical Council (GPhC). This body, since 2010, has been the 'regulatory' authority for all pharmacists. Since the last date on which I had actually practised, was as far back as 2005, it is unlikely that I will ever be entitled to practice as pharmacist again.

The amount, and nature, of the work I would have to do, and the corroborating evidence that I would need to obtain and retain, makes the prospect an un duly onerous one.

I regret this very much, and I do miss practice in my old profession.

The last position that I occupied as a pharmacist was as manager of a small community pharmacy in Swansea. It was situated towards the edge of the busy city centre and I had heard about it via the trusty, old, pharmacist's 'bush telegraph'. An established pharmacist had come across the opportunity to expand his involvement in the profession by buying a new new premises in a small shopping parade. He needed someone to manage the business. Was I interested?

The hours were less onerous than my last job, there were no late nights, no regular Sundays and it was 10 miles or so closer to home. It was to be a family run business. Of COURSE I was interested.

Thus, began my 2 year professional stint in Swansea.

The shop was very nice, the members of staff were very pleasant and each was entirely professional in discharging their duties.

The only regular, full time, member of staff was the proprietor's wife. I liked her very much and we seemed to get along perfectly fine. Yet, I sensed all might not have been well with her in her home life. None of my business of course, but I could not do anything but empathise with her. The shop, as a new-ish venture was not phenomenally busy. My feelings were, that it was a 'comfortable' workload. The local doctors, their receptionists and ancillary staff were also very pleasant and, there was an extent to which this should have provided a satisfying and rewarding existence.

But, I have always been a rather restless soul. Pretty soon, I was bored.

I had been reading about the existence of a well known, and local, college of further education that offered a range of part-time studies leading to recognised qualifications.

After, not much, thought, I decided to enrol on the part time, external University of London LL.B. course.

For a time over that summer of 1993, I was like a youngster on Christmas morning! I sent for and received, the course's overall syllabus and also, the individual course subject's written tuition guides complete with suggested reading lists and sample exam questions.

But, it would mean that I would have to take an onerous, and circuitous route back to practice.

MY YEAR LONG SOJOURN TO THE BAR VOCATIONAL COURSE, AND MY SUBSEQUENT YEARS IN LEGAL PRACTICE.

*I*n 1996, and with the blessing, both of my dear parents, and Maria, I made a second professional 'debut' when I decided to join 'The Honourable Society of The Middle Temple' as a student member, with a view to eventually being called to the Bar of England and Wales. [Note that Scotland has its own separate Bar to Wales and England. This is because, unlike England or Wales, the legal system is based on the notion of a 'Common Law' rather than in 'Roman Law' as in most of the rest of Europe. The USA is another country whose legal system is based on 'Common Law'.

So, at the start of the 1996/97 academic year, I went off to study at the Inns of Court School of Law (ICSL).

My father had kindly, covered the course tuition fees for the whole year-long course of lectures, tutorials, and practical classes.

I would be paying for my accommodation, food, and all the other day to day costs and expenses of my attendance such as my clothing. I would also be undertaking to contribute toward the upkeep, including rental of our state - of - the art bungalow in a place called Pentregwenlais (which is just off the Llandeilo to Swansea trunk Road) of Maria, Rhys and Sian and 'Nalah' our family's pet cat.

As far as my accommodation for the first term of the course was concerned, Maria had arranged for me to stay with her elderly Uncle Albert and his partner 'Sal' who lived very close to South Woodford Central Line tube station. So it would be ideal for me to commute, on a daily basis, to Chancery Lane(also on the Central Line) for the school, which was in Grays Inn Place. WC2.

ICSL

I well remember attending the ICSL, which was much bigger than The School of Pharmacy. For a start, the student numbers were much higher at ICSL. The yearly intake was around 1,000; The School of Pharmacy just around 100. True. That that was a 3 year long degree course, so the number in daily attendance at the school was around 300 undergraduates. ICSL courses were intended to be just a year long per student, so that puts the figure of 1,000 in a totally different league. At ICSL, I, like all other students, were there to participate in the 'Bar Vocational Course' or the 'BVC' in its shortened, initialled version.

As one of the more mature students on the BVC, (I was already 35 years of age) My initial thoughts were that it was refreshing to be back in the company of people who were nearly 15 years my juniors.

It's true that ICSL students were spread over all the spectrum of ages, from early 20s for the youngest, up to people in their early or mid 50s before reading for the Bar. Some, like me, had already had careers in other disciplines. They had also come from a much wider demographic than the Pharmacy students that I studied with.

For example, there were many Americans, Canadians, Indians, Pakistanis, Afghans, and even one Peruvian that I recall.

The School of Pharmacy had a much larger proportion of students from the Asian subcontinent including, South East Asians. Strangely, to my eyes, there seemed to be almost no South East Asian trainees or students at the BVC.

I started to feel very mixed emotions about being away from Maria, Sian and Rhys during my time at ICSL.

I missed my family and my family life so much while I was away.

I tried to involve myself in as much of the student activities as was practicable or possible.

I even turned out for a couple of appearances for the Rugby team.

A match had been arranged against the Bar. Although they, like ourselves, were very much a 'scratch' side, they had some good, experienced individuals in their side. As our BVC side were principally made up of men still in their early 20s, the Bar team were around 10 years older per man and their squad seemed a lot more organised as a result. The outcome was, that they beat us very comfortably. I forget the exact score, but they won by around a 20 to 30 points margin!

My second appearance was against Nottingham University Law School. A coach had been arranged for us to make the 100 or so mile one way trip. We lost. But it was a memorable trip, particularly for several of our team's members who themselves had been Nottingham University graduates before joining the BVC.

At the end of that Michaelmas term, we would all be examined on our learned knowledge of the law and procedure.

The pass mark to be able to remain on the course was 70%. Those who failed to make the grade would have to leave the course. I was determined to achieve the pass mark, but, unlike my previous exam attempts, there were no such things as compendia of past papers, student guides or even 'Mug Up' materials. The exam format would be 'Multiple Choice' of answers to legal and situational problems were given. But only 1 of 4 possibilities or 'answers' would earn any marks.

Out of the 4 possible answer suggestions given; only one would earn marks against the 70% required.

One of the 4 suggestions would obviously be wrong; another would be the right answer. Each of the remaining 2 choices would be plausible, but were either wrong, or not what the examiners were looking for.

The point was; it was thought to be impossible to succeed in the exam by pure chance or by luck. You HAD to know the law!

It was NOW, that the rather abstract nature of many of the tutorial and lecture contents made true sense.

I did the closed book exam, finished my paper and went home to my family for Christmas.

We were not due back at ICSL until several days into January 1997. That is when we would each learn whether we had passed or failed.

It was, therefore, a rather muted, and tense mood for me over that 3 and a bit week holiday.

Albert and Sally had decided that they were not going to offer me a place to stay for the Spring term at ICSL. I can't say that I was surprised. I was not much of a house guest for them; irregular hours, one or two absences, and Albert, for one, did not appear to be a man who liked conversation.

We had virtually nothing in common, He was an old soldier, a 'Squaddie' type, no interest in football, rugby or cricket and most of my time at their house. He was very kind toward me, but I quite understood the position.

Although 'Sal' was almost the total opposite to Albert in demeanour, bright, outgoing, sociable and easy company, she had a very limited outlook beyond her WFH job of sorting widgets for a local firm. After cooking dinner for me and Albert, she spent every evening WFH by sorting through masses of widgets but, to the exclusion of everything else.

Therefore, I would be leaving South Woodford for the final time as a resident over the Christmas/ New Year holiday 1996/7 and looking for somewhere else to act as a base, stay and live.

I had visions of having to either find a new place 'ab initio' or, face the daunting prospect of contacting a place in the Newbury Park are of Ilford where I had spent a few nights during previous visits to London from Pentregwenlais.

Maria must very kindly have pulled some strings on my behalf over that period.

She announced that her parents, John and Ella Nottage had agreed that I could spend the Spring term lodging with them in Kelvedon Hatch, just outside Brentwood in Essex.

That was great news, I immediately recalled the many happy times I had spent at their house since I first started courting Maria.

So, I once again, found myself embarking on what was by now, a familiar car journey between South Wales and mid- Essex.

1997 should prove to be a landmark year. I SHOULD be able to get a lucrative job or a secure tenancy if I passed the BVC, I still retained my status as a pharmacist locum, I still retained my old pharmacy contacts and I still belonged to the same Locum Agencies and would continue to do so for some time yet, if, for any reason, I did not succeed on the BVC. After all, I believed that I was a diligent and reliable person and I was even covering regular evening shifts at a multiple pharmacy in South Norwood, South London to top up my income and try and cover the costs of raising our 1 income family during this crucial period.

Unfortunately I had also succumbed to an impulse to affirm my masculinity. Over just a few weeks. That's all. But I had an 'affair' between the last week in November and the first three weeks of December 1996.

I had noticed a very attractive lady mooching around after lectures and tutorials during the latter part of that term. One day, I decided to try and engage her in conversation. What I should have done, was to either to completely ignore her, or, if I couldn't do that, then just say an off - hand 'Good day' or, 'How are you?' or 'Nice weather we're having , isn't it?'

Instead we got chatting and soon, I was offering to share a cup of coffee at break times and the like.

Firstly, I learnt that her name was Lucinda.

She was petite, blonde, and I thought, rather modestly under dressed.

I discovered that she actually lived, during the times we were not at ICSL, in a town on the South Coast near the English Channel. She would spend all week in London so that she could attend the course at the ICSL, but would then travel back on the weekends back to her home on the south coast.

One Friday around this time, we sat next to each other at a morning session lecture. At the ensuing coffee break, coffee break, we sat together. She leaned over to me and whispered into my ear: 'Do you want to come home with me tonight?'

I fell for it!

'Oh Yes please!' I said.

After all, it would not have been my first night away from Albert and Sally's; there had been the weekend with the rugby team in Nottingham too. Maria and the children were safely at home, over 200 miles away.

So, I gambled that, I could have some fun AND get away with it. I may have been proposing something rather immoral, but Hey! It was not an actual crime, was it?

Lucinda re assured me that, although she had a regular, live in, boyfriend, he would be away himself that week - on some work related, or academic conference, or something! So she and I were not going to be disturbed. And I could get a train back to London on Sunday evening; she, apparently, had no lectures or work at ICSL on the Monday, so she would travel back later, on her own!

It goes, almost without saying, that we both had a fantastic time that weekend!!.

But, subsequently, it also affirmed the truism that 'There is no such thing as a free lunch'. I would live to pay dearly for that stolen weekend during the weeks and months that followed.

At Michaelmas break itself, I went back to Pentregwenlais, as planned, and then spent Christmas Day and the rest of the holidays, as planned too. I even sneaked some discreet phone calls off to Lucinda to check that she was having a good Christmas break too. But, of course, I would have to drive back to my next destination, which was John and Ella's house before the Spring term began during the first week in January.

Before I drove back, I made sure I looked in on Sian and Rhys separately to say "Goodbye" to them; by which, of course, I meant; 'au revoir' This would prove to be one of the last times ever, that we would all be a 'family' in the implicit sense of that description, and not just in it's actual, legal sense, but also, it's more romantic or spiritual meaning! I began to drive. I left the bungalow's attached driveway, steered the car down the steep downward hill, turned right on to the main Swansea to Llandeilo trunk road, all the familiar parts of the route, past the 'Red Lion' pub and the little parade of shops. I drove over the, by now, familiar route; in the direction of the first junction of the M4 motorway (junction number 49), at a place called 'Pont Abraham'. I had taken that route pretty much every working day since we, as a family had come to Wales, to live, way back in early 1991. But THIS time, for the first time ever, and, as all the subsequent journeys came, and went, I cried. In fact, I blubbed! Uncontrollably! The prosaic reason was that I had only, minutes earlier, said 'Goodbye' to 5 year old Rhys on my way out of the house. His response? THAT was what was making me so upset. He barely turned to me, but said:'Yeah daddy, see you next Spring'. The words were said with such nonchalance, and so matter-of-factly that they had made me wonder what on earth I was doing by abandoning my family!

All along, I must have been kidding myself that what I was doing by becoming, in effect, a perpetual student was all for the best. All for the good of my family too. I was overcome with tearful emotion not just for those prosaic reasons, but also because, only a few weeks earlier, I had been wantonly cheating on my wife, with Lucinda and by taking advantage of my absence from Pentregwenlais, my home, in order to do so!

The episode of tearfulness did not last THAT long, as once I was back on the Eastbound, carriageway of the M4, my normal reactions to driving that familiar, but lengthy route returned quickly, as if somehow by reflex action, and I had soon dried my eyes so that I could concentrate on the busy, 200 - plus miles of road and its driving conditions again.

So, by that night in early January of 1997, I again pulled my car into John and Ella's driveway to embark on the next and hopefully, ante- penultimate episode of my quest for a lucrative career at the Bar.

As usual after a long drive, I did not socialise very well. I preferred to take an early night. Maybe read a few lines of whatever book a might then have been ploughing through, the drift of to sleep in preparation for my next day's reading of sections of the BVC material.

There was a vast amount of material to get through before one could even dream of successfully completing the course.

The material was presented in the form of written 'Manuals' on a large range of subject areas covering each topic that was included in the course's syllabus.

The manuals covered the substantive law and the legal procedures applicable to as many areas of a Barrister's day to day work as it was possible to squeeze in to a 500 or so page of A4 paper soft back book.

There were separate manuals for each of what were deemed to be the 'core' topics on the BVC. These, in short, were along the lines of 'What EVERY barrister needs to know.......'.

There were also manuals covering a range of topics dealing with; 'What every barristrer OUGHT to know' And there were a series of manuals covering specialist areas of the law of which we, as individuals, would be making a selection for study in the final term of the BVC which would take place during the 1997 summer term.

The 'Core' topics to be studied, and mastered were: Evidence, Advocacy, Criminal Law and Procedure, Civil Law and Procedure, (legal) Opinion writing, Drafting (of legal documents covering such things as claims, defences to claims, requests for further and better particulars of one's opponent's claims, and schedules of losses, claims in rebuttal of losses and the like,) In fact, the BVC seemed to be aiming to cover absolutely everything and anything that any PUPIL barrister would need to be able to do, do automatically, and do to a professional;s standard.

In addition, we students had to select a further 2 practice areas for study during the 3rd term. If any of us as BVC trainees had a particular ambition to follow these topics as their career choice, then this was the opportunity to study that particular subject/topic in the detail necessary to undertake a pupillage in it.

My choices turned out to be; Employment Law in practice, and Consumer Law and Credit (arrangements) in practice.

Because I had recently studied an Employment Law module during my LL.B. degree at Swansea Institute, and that 'consumer' law and credit seemed very topical, (what, with the television programmes such as 'That's Life', BBC's 'Nationwide' (now covered by the prime time 7pm 'The One Show') and the Martin Lewis money advice programme on ITV) it could prove to be a lucrative area of practice for me in the future..

As it turned out, in my actual practice, these two were pretty ambitious choices. Both were oversubscribed and really required me to have contacts, especially solicitors, on board who would send me regular work. Pupillages were difficult to secure in general, and the spring term at ICSL was beginning to turn into an endless round of interviews with Barrister's Chambers, all of which would end in rejection!

As the Bar training's 'Vocational' stage, the BVC was designed to get one to the first stage of being able to practice. This was known as 'Pupillage' where a person who had succeeded on the BVC could apply to become the 'Pupil' of a barrister who was already established in practice. If the 'Pupil' got through THAT stage, he she could practice on they're own as soon as that, effectively, a probation period had ended. Typically, such a barrister would choose whether to work in an employment situation e.g. in the legal department of a local authority, a large or small firm, preferably, of solicitors, or perhaps a Law Centre, or Citizens Advice bureau, a Charity or some other type of agency, firm, or employer who could send me legal advocacy work.. The alternative was to work alone as a 'Sole practitioner' OR, to join what was known as a 'Set' also known as Barrister's 'Chambers'.

So, for example, if a BVC trainee wished to become a criminal barrister and so, be able to prosecute, or defend, cases in the criminal Courts, be they Magistrates or Crown Courts, he or she would have, firstly, to succeed on the BVC, then become an already practising barrister's 'pupil' then finally, practice on they're own account, either by joining a suitable firm, as above, or a set of chambers. Only then could they, he, or she be allowed to have un- limited rights of audience in an English (or Welsh) Court room.

Within a few days, I would be back to equally familiar surroundings at ICSL, BUT, something had also changed. And, very much for the worse!............

1997.

As I pulled my car in to John and Ella's driveway, the daylight had long ago vanished, to be replaced by the dismal gloom of an early January evening.

The reception I got from my hosts this time, was one of urbanity; in contrast with the open arms, hugs and kisses of the years since Maria and me had first visited the house, some 11 or so, years earlier.

I felt tired myself after firstly, the emotion and upset of leaving the Pentregwenlais bungalow, Maria, Sian and Rhys yet again . Secondly, the length of the car journey to Essex itself, but also, thirdly, my sense of inner guilt, knowing that the way I had behaved was inimical to a happy, married, family lifestyle. I couldn't see how Maria had seemed to, just, know that I had been un faithful, but the change in her attitude to me since December was notable, and palpable.

Somehow, I thought, she HAD found out. But having racked my brains, I could not work out the mechanism of HOW this could have happened, or, HOW MUCH she actually knew!

John and Ella were always very nice to me. After all, I was a son-in-law of theirs. But, also, after all, I had broken the trust of their daughter Maria over a stupid affair which had, effectively, only lasted for a few days.

That night, I went to bed as soon as I could. But I most definitely, had mixed feelings about what tomorrow, and the Spring term, would hold. True, I would be back in the familiar groove of the BVC, with its incessant reading of materials, case preparation and even, the trick of locating the appropriate classroom for my next lesson or tutorial;and in the banter and discussion amongst the dozen or so other students that comprised my tutorial group.

When I walked in to Grays Inn place, the usual mass of day one of a new term's students seemed to be there. But I could not find Lucinda. Not an immediate cause for panic to me; there were many other potentially reasonable explanations for her absence. Maybe she had just not been able to return from home her yet? Maybe she had contracted a heavy cold, or the 'Flu, or food poisoning!. Or maybe, there had been some family emergency, or a bereavement, or SOMETHING!

To put general matters into the context of those times, I had only just received my very first mobile telephone handset as a birthday present from Maria; only 3 weeks previously. But, this was still in 1997. It was not the present day! If truth be told, I hadn't yet worked out how to use this 'new-fangled' technology. Nowadays? Of course;No problem! Seemingly everyone has Smartphones today, and they have endless lists of 'contacts' on their microchip SIM cards. They can call up news bulletins, send and receive Emails or even Download full movies if the wish using their Smartphone.

Back then, 28 years ago, things were not that straightforward.

Maybe she would be in at ICSL tomorrow? I knew she hadn't been asked to leave the course for any reason. The 'Bush Telegraph' worked in my favour to ensure that. As things were, many of the 1,000 or so students HAD either been asked, or had been forced, to do so and leave the BVC for a variety of reasons or motives. The key to be able to stay on the BVC course, was simply, to do well in the exams and assessments. The potential reasons for absence or, for not being present on any given day obviously varied: things such as long-term illness, lack of aptitude, too much pressure, not what was hoped for when starting the course; All the above were common reasons for abandoning the course.

But not for me! And not, on the face of things; for Lucinda.

She DID attend the course again, towards the end of that first week. But, from then on, she appeared to be trying to avoid any contact with me.

I felt somewhat downhearted, if not, a little bewildered. Yes, I was still able to do my course work and any of it's attendant preparation. But for the first time in my living memory, I felt depressed. The standard of work required was as hard as ever. There were comparatively few opportunities for entertainment or distractions from the drudgery of that early spring term. Even my Inn's programme of dining fixtures for the forthcoming Spring term seemed decidedly un- inspiring.

Un - daunted; I suppose a bit like an old trooper, I 'Soldiered' on.

I had been finding it hard, as well as expensive to continue to commute to and from John and Ella's 5 times a week, every week. Fortunately, during the duration of the course so far, I had become friendly with another person on the BVC, a chap called 'Pete'. He was not in the same tutorial groups as me. But through things like chatting to each other over our daily coffee breaks and, our being of similar ages and demographic backgrounds, we hit it off.

A common meeting place for the students on the course was the ICSL's own Cafe, on the Grays Inn Place site.

The cafe was, rather prosaically, called 'Adjourments', and was open only to ICSL's students and whichever members of the course staff happened to wander in from time to time.

Pete himself was married with a young, teenaged family. He lived in an affluent, London suburb which, apparently, he had inherited from his late parents as their only child.

As we were chatting during on of our daily tea/coffee breaks, Pete mentioned that we would be prepared to let one of his bedrooms to me on very reasonable terms.

We made a deal, and so, for the third time in 3 terms, I was on the move again.

Pete and I kept in touch for many years from the end of our time on the BVC. But he, like me, had other 'strings to his bow'. I was still a pharmacist, still doing occasional pharmacy locum work and Pete was still involved in financial services.

So, on a personal level at least, we would have no reason not to get on.

In fact, I enjoyed every minute of my time while lodging at Pete's house.

He recommended the novels of John Grisham to me. And, once I had read one or two, I was a devotee. Historically, I had never devoted much time, or effort, to reading works of fiction. I loved reading about facts, whether scientific, or histories, or even religious accounts such as are found in the Christian Bible.

I found the John Grisham books to be a relatively easy read.

Every night at Pete's house, I would be sure to read a couple of Chapters of a John Grisham novel before dozing off to sleep.

Meanwhile, we were both aware that the BVCs final, 'Make or Break' assessments were approaching.

I felt I had always struggled with one of the core course topics called 'Advocacy'. One day, while I was wandering around the Notice Board area at ICSL, I noticed an announcement that an Actor, who was 'Interested in the law', would make himself available to try to assist any student who was struggling with the coursework or tutorials dealing with 'Advocacy'.

In those days, The ICSL was very closely involved with a nearby Acting School from central London.

In fact, deputations of their students would be assigned to collaborate on the various practical sessions which were held in conjunction with our Civil, and Criminal Litigation tutorials. They would play the parts of us student's clients, witnesses or even court staff or members of the public during the respective practical sessions.

Advocacy, put quite simply, is the art of communication' that is, having the skill and ability to get your message across, to be understood and to be heard. Your Advocacy could be in written form or in Verbal form, visual form, oral form, aural form or pictorial; whatever the sender, or 'Advocate' deemed to be appropriate or practicable for the task in hand.

I jumped at the suggestion, and so I signed up expressing my interest in getting this Actor's help.

With the sheer volume of work now to be accomplished to ensure success on the BVC, I must admit to having forgotten all about my request for his help!

One day, a member of the ICSL's front of house staff reminded me of my commitment and said that this Actor had had a long journey from his home, had got several people to 'see' but would accommodate me there and then! She told me where he was waiting and so, would I please hurry up! When I got to the relevant room and knocked on the door, I honestly had no idea what I was letting myself in for. The fact that, by all accounts, it was I who had asked for this meeting was lost on me in the heat of this moment.

I don't know whether this actor was linked with the actor's school, or what his antecedents were, but, with hindsight, it was the best that COULD have happened to me at that point in time.

He was able to supply me with what I had really been needing.That was; simple self confidence!

First, he asked me to talk about myself as if I were introducing myself to him, as a stranger. Secondly, he asked me to speak in favour of anything I liked. Absolutely anything! Nothing would be off-limits;

Finally, he asked me to speak AGAINST any topic, notion or idea. Again, the actual subject matter would be entirely my choice!

I cannot now remember what I spoke about in any of those 3 broad categories. But, by the end of our short session, I was 'rabbiting' away in the manner of any of the great orators in history.

In hort, I had 'Got my MoJo' back.

So, bolstered by this boost to my personal armoury of skills and aptitudes, I reckoned that I was able to again set foot in to the big, wide world and do myself justice. Now, to finish the BVC, look for a pupillage and then, if all went well, commence practice as 'Learned Counsel', a barrister in independent practice.

Comparatively little else of note stands out in mind about the the final period of my stay on the BVC.

There were still 1 or 2 dining sessions left for me to attend.

The institution of 'dining' goes back all the way to the foundation of each of the 4 separate 'Inns of Court' during mediaeval times. For myself, as a student member of The Honourable Society of the Middle Temple, I was bound, as a condition of membership, to comply with their rules and customs.

From the fourteenth century, student barristers have used the experience of dining for the purposes of furthering their legal education, socialising, meeting with other members of Society and complying with the customs, terms and conditions of Inn membership.

All those desiring to be called to the Bar and acquire practising rights had to attend a total of 18 dinners during the length of the course. As with any meal, there was a cost involved. Although my late father had already paid the £5,000 in course fees on my behalf, this did not include any of the prices of the 18 dining sessions that I had impliedly wanted.

Dining was a pastime that I would heartily recommend to any member of the public as a a 'One - Off' experience.

For fully qualified barristers with they're own already established practices, it is an excellent and entertaining way to meet friends, colleagues, associates and even family members in what is for all those, an informal situation.

It is a way of being entertained; during my time on the BVC, guests at the 'Music; dinners included a recital, in Middle Temple Hall by the Russian concert pianist Dimitri Horostovsky, Also, a 'Jazz' night with the band leader Humphrey Lyttleton, whose wider family had been involved with establishment of Port Talbot steelworks way back in the inter-war Britain of the 1920s and 1930s.

There were the so-called 'Moot' nights, totally informal debating nights, 'ordinary' dining nights and, a Christmas term time 'Revels' night where the 'Lord of Misrule' was notionally hosting!

For the barrister him, or her self, it is a recognised, and valuable, way to spend an evening entertaining those friends, colleagues, associates or family close to them.

For Bar students, it is enjoyable, albeit compulsory, part of training for the bar. For everyone else, if you ever get the opportunity to Dine at one of the Inns of Court, do so!

Invariably served with dinner, are carafes of Port. It is easy to get very drunk. Traditionally, dining was seen as a form of tuition that emphasises the art of being able to discipline one self in the company of one's guests. Keeping this in mind,

The cost of a ticket in my day, varied between about £25 for ordinary dining to about £40 for the higher profile Dimitri Horostovsky or Humphrey Lyttlelton gigs. With inflation, the price nowadays is around £60 per dinner.

Rarely, one would get to dine with others from my tutorial group, but mainly, the other students would book alone because the BVC was such a busy way of life, that this would have been impracticable type of existence for virtually anyone else on the course.

As the number of my eaten dinners approached the target of 18, it was time to start thinking about 'Call Night' itself.

Traditionally, a new Barrister could be formally called at one of 4 'call nights' . These are: 'Hilary', 'Trinity', 'Deferred Trinity', and 'Michaelmas' reflecting the ecclesiastical seasons used by the Anglican Church. From a practical point of view, almost all my colleagues and fellow students on the BVC chose the first available date after finishing the BVC. That meant, the 'Deferred Trinity' call in my case.

As my own BVC course assessment had been ranked as 'Competent', (rather than, 'Very competent' or, even 'Outstanding'), I was entitled to be called to the Bar at whichever of those dates was most convenient.

I therefore chose the 'Deferred Trinity' call which, had already been fixed by The Middle Temple Inn for 8th October 1997.

My guests would be both my parents who, naturally, would want to make the journey from Port Talbot for the ceremony and stay in London overnight too.

Most of the successful candidates in my year or in my old tutorial group also chose the Deferred Trinity call. Those, I could expect to see, and talk to them, perhaps for the final time; or, even meet their families. But for some of my erstwhile associates, colleagues or friends, it would not be convenient to come on 8th October, for instance, if they would have to travel from a foreign country, or their friends family or loved ones were not available that night, or, they weren't free because if work et cetera.

Meanwhile, my hunt for a pupillage went on.

I calculate that more than half of those in my my tutorial group had, by then, secured a pupillage. Of course, one only NEEDED to have done so if one wanted to to be able to appear as an advocate in court, or otherwise hold oneself out as a practising Barrister.

In my case, I could always just go back to being a community pharmacist get a job, or continue - locum - ing.

PUPILLAGE ODDYSEYS

For a while, though, that is what I ended up doing.

Towards the end of 1992, I was made aware that a pharmacist's job was going to become available, for a fixed, 2 - year duration and at a very lucrative rate of pay.

The position was the most onerous one that I could have envisaged. The hours were; Mondays to Fridays between 9am and 7pm, 9 until 6pm on Saturdays , and, a 1 hour's chemist 'Rota' duty every Sunday from 12 midday until 1pm. In other words, effectively a 7 day week! It was in a nearby town to where my parents were living and, with Maria, I calculated it COULD be done but, instead of commuting the 60-odd mile return trip every day, I would stay at my parent's house on one regular weeknight, maybe 2, to break the week up and also, to be able to give Maria a bit of a rest on those weeknights too.

In reality, the stint actually worked very well. However, at times of strain, I reminded myself that it WAS, a fixed contract; it WOULD come to an end, and we would take stock and see where our respective futures lay thereafter.

Maria was always very proud that I was a qualified pharmacist, in regular work, and earning good money.

BUT she was also very keen on my pursuit of a pupillage. 'You've come so far' she would say; 'it would be a shame to waste all that effort now'.

I had been writing letters and/or leaving messages to local chambers telling them 1) I was available, and 2) Please could I have a pupillage? type communications. But, so far, all to no avail!

I would now have to take the latest step in an ever increasing list of 'Look at Yourself' self analyses, and decide what I really wanted to do! Who I would want to BE for the rest of my life; or, at least, during my WORKING life years! I was then just 35 years old. I should still have between 25 and

35 years' of useful working life left before 'calling it a day'. I would want to do my best for Maria, Sian and Rhys throughout, since of course, I must have seemed to be just a 'perpetual student' to them.

One evening, while I was at home, I got an unexpected telephone call. It was from the leader of the Wales and Chester circuit!

The message was short, and to the point: 'Give ** a ring' he said; 'He'll be expecting a call from you……….'.

I rang back straight away,. It was the head of a local Barrister's chambers in Swansea. 'I've heard you want a pupillage' the caller said. 'Do you want 6 months or 12 months?'.

'Oh' …..I mumbled….'Six….I suppose'.

In hindsight, a could, and probably should, have said '12'.

But, my naturally conservative nature got the better of me.

There was a large part of that conservativeness that did not want to tie myself to any commitment that might prove unwise. So, six moths it would be!

The following evening, after court hearings and 'Wash-Up' had finished for the day, I drove the 20 so miles from my home, to chambers to meet the members of the chambers 'Pupillage committee'; those barrister members of chambers who were assigned to ensure that Chambers would always hire the best people for Pupillage. The advantage of this approach is that if a star of the legal practitioner firmament is ready, willing and available, then they ought to be signed up without demur. If they are young and are treated well, they will be an asset for years to come

The interview went very well. The Pupillage committee were suitably impressed by my academic record, my professional record in community and hospital pharmacy, my 'CV' and my overall character. They were happy to accept me as the 'new pupil' along with another young lady whom I recall, was coming straight from law school via mainstream education but had been interested in a full, 12 month Pupillage. She was, of course, much younger than me.

The entire process had had a refreshing air of informality and so, I decided it would be in order for me to accept my 6 months, then apply for a further 'six' if things went well, or simply look for another et of chambers for my second six moths, or try and get a law related job somewhere, or just do something else (including going back to full time pharmacy if need be). Ever the optimist, I considered the world to be my oyster!

So, I took my first physical steps in to chambers one weekday morning in lat-ish 1997. Firstly, I introduced myself to cambers' chief clerk who, in turn, made introductions to each of the half dozen or so junior clerks (at least, to those who happened to be at work, in chambers on that day).

I was then taken around to meet as many of the tenants as happened to be present. I tried to remember as many of their names as possible and also, what their particular areas of expertise were.

Of all the various legal disciplines covered in chambers as a whole, I was most interested in clinal law. There was no specialist for pharmacy law. There WAS a medically qualified Doctor who had 'Medical Negligence' as her area of specialty, but most others were 'General Common Law' practitioners who, typically, would turn their hands to any piece of work that came their way; in line with the 'Cab Rank Rule'; the rule of conduct that states that any barrister in independent practice would take the next case in line PROVIDED it was within his, or her, area of competence.

This rule is designed to prevent barristers, particularly those at the more junior levels of expertise, from refusing to act for lay clients on spurious grounds; or simply on the basis that they are lower down in the waiting list for a barrister's services. Examples of such spurious grounds might be a client's personal characteristics such as their political views, their physical appearance or such other 'Protected characteristics' as their age, gender, sexuality, nationality, Ill health, or a 'neurodiversity' e.g. autism or cerebral palsy.

The system is designed to work in a way that unconscious biases are done away with.

So, that initial tour and 'meet the team' session on my first day in chambers was very informative. But the nature of working in chambers meant that, while I was being shown around chambers by an already established practitioner, other barrister were out at court hearings client conferences or simply 'not to be disturbed' in the library, or even, on their 'day off' from work.

I looked forward to getting the chance to meet any others over the next days, weeks and months until, either my 6 months was over, or, I managed to stay on as chambers' pupil, or moved somewhere else.

It was during this time that I experienced my first taste of an alleged 'Murder' case. Head of chambers had been given a brief for acting as the junior prosecutor to a member of the senior bar in that case, and he wanted me to establish the chronology of the events as fully as possible.

I was delighted at being given that opportunity, and as a pupil, it was memorable for being the first time that I could be trusted to establish my own methodology and time-frame for the task. I decided the best way to do so would be to work towards producing a written report covering the murder itself, initial report, details of the case investigation, its sad outcome, and anything else that might be useful to my head of chambers as junior prosecutor in the case.

Normally, the hierarchy of the Bar is sided into 'Juniors' and more senior members of the profession. Usually, the senior members will have   'taken silk' and, in those days would be entitled to use the initials 'QC' after their names. Since the death of HM Queen Elizabeth II and the resulting accession of HM King Charles III to the throne, senior counsel who have taken silk may use the designation 'KC' after their names.

Of course, I had the professional backstop of the safety net, that, as a pupil, my work WOULD be supervised by my 'Pupil master', a more senior junior member of chambers who had agreed to so act.

As far as the murder case preparation was concerned, I would be able to take my work home and there was no formal deadline given to me for its completion (at least not at that stage). But, the initial court appearance was imminent and, a few days later, I learned that the accused had indicated in a preliminary hearing that he was going to plead 'NOT Guilty' upon his arraignment, which was set for a few days later.

A feature of the Common law system used in England and Wales and other common law jurisdictions throughout the world is that the prosecution must prove the case against any accused person 'Beyond reasonable doubt'. It is a high standard, and ensures the dangers of an accusation made agains any citizen does not produce a miscarriage of justice. Put another way; it protects against any innocent person from being convicted and thereby facing punishment by being fined, imprisoned or otherwise losing their liberty. For example someone sentenced to a 'Community Order' will lose their freedom to come, and go, as they please and will always be subject to a period under the compulsory direction of the probation service. For example, they maybe subject of an order to do unpaid work, or be under a curfew restricting their right to be out of their homes at any time.

So, any accused person pleading 'Not Guilty' in court then puts the PROSECUTION in the position that they MUST prove their case 'beyond reasonable doubt' to establish the guilt of the accused person.

As soon as the piece of work that head of chambers had wanted my to do was over, I then found myself back on Chamber's treadmill and there would be no 'Happy Ending' to my brush with a serious criminal allegation. Instead, I would be taking the next piece work in the clerk's diary.

They had a a lot of instructions in relation to road traffic matters; from insurance companies assessment of vehicle damage after road traffic accidents (RTAs), to drivers appealing their convictions for speeding; the Police, prosecuting such drivers and, my favourite type of case, the valuation of damages to be paid for persons injured as a result of having been involved in an RTA. Rarely, of course, involvement in an RTA had resulted in a participant's death or serious injury and the only practical legal remedy for the victim or victims would be some sort of award of monetary damages to be assessed by the court.

Naturally, that type of assessment straddled the police duties, the actions of any police officers who were, or became, involved, insurance company assessments, photographic and/or CCTV recordings, eye witness accounts and often, what an accused person him or her self had said about the incident, perhaps in a formal police taped interview after the events in question and before any charge(s) were proffered.

I estimate, that over my years as a criminal barrister (over 25 at the last count), not far from half my general common law work related to road traffic matters of one kind, or another.

TROUBLE AT HOME?

$\mathcal{I}$ have always been a creature of habit. For example, when getting dressed, I alway put my left shoe on first in the morning; I always eat my meals by consuming any vegetables first, and only then, moving on to the meat or fish portions; I always follow the same routines on waking; Everything 'HAS it's place' and 'Everything IN it's place'. I hated any; what I would think of, as unjustified variations to my well established routines.

I was accustomed, not just to working, but also by leaving the house each day, taking the same route to work in the car, parking in the same space on arrival, making a cup of tea as soon as I walked over the threshold, et cetera, et cetera.

On getting home at the end of each working day, I would follow the exact, same, sequence of events in reverse.

I was, in fact, deluding myself that this was all perfectly normal. Wasn't it what everybody else did?

After all; didn't EVERYBODY call in at the local pub for a 'quick half' after work on Friday evenings? Didn't they then expect to be served a dinner consisting of a large, breaded plaice, oven - style chips and portion of garden peas for 'Dinner'? Didn't they all park their cars at home, say 'Hello' to their children, welcome the baby sitter for the evening, then escort their wives back to the same pub for the same aperitif, then go to the same curry house in town, arriving at the same time, order the same favourite, well tried and trusted dishes, including starter, main, and pudding?

That much may be true. But, of course, it had the effect of turning me into a really, rather boring, individual.

I believe that over time, this boring and entirely predictable existence played a role in the break up of my marriage. In short, Maria had recently started 'Playing around'!

While I was spending so much of my time at work, on courses, or on stays away from home of varying lengths, Maria had been STUCK at home. She must have felt imprisoned. She is a naturally rather gregarious person, like her late dad was. I know she was spending a lot of time during the periods that I was at work, or 'away', chatting to the other mothers from Sian's school, comparing notes and gossiping about their domestic existences.

One Friday night, while I was still a first term student at ICSL, I decided, on a whim, to surprise Maria, Sian and Rhys by going back to our house in Pentregwenlais by way of a weekend visit.

Instead of using the car, I thought my surprise visit would have as much impact if I travelled on a National Express bus from Victoria Coach station and asked the driver for a return ticket to my nearest stop, then, I could get a Taxi back to home. I would then have to do the same journey back on the following Sunday evening, which, I knew, would depart from Swansea Quadrant bus station.

The outward journey went like clockwork. I quietly put the front door key in the lock, turned it gently, and tip toed in. I knew Maria was there. The lights were on and, why should she not be there?

When I got to the lounge entrance , Maria was sat, drink in hand, with her back to me, watching the TV. I said nothing. But, just looking at that scenario; and memorising it during over 25 years, I was struck by its plaintive SADNESS!

Maria's face brightened as soon as she saw me, and she as soon as she had, oriented herself to the fact of my unexpected, and unanticipated presence, we managed to settle down to planning what to do with the limited time I had over that weekend, before I would have to return to ICSL lectures and coursework for first thing Monday morning.

At a practical level, that would mean having to leave Pentregwenlais for ICSL at around 5am on a Monday morning, to have chance of making a 9am session in Grays Inn place! Or, I would be stuck with the alternative of travelling back to London during the Sunday early evening.

I almost invariably chose the latter of those 2 options.

In fact, I remember only 1 occasion where I decided on the former. What, with being caught in the Monday rush hour traffic coming in to London and it's environs, I STILL failed to make it to ICS on that occasion until most of the Monday morning had gone!

So, really, neither option was satisfactory.

Even When Maria became aware of my unexpected presence. I, of course, in my arrogance, treated my arrival as just a case of 'water off a duck's back'.

But, as it turned out, we all had a delightful weekend in each other's company.

A favourite pastime for our family, when time was short, was to visit Carreg Cennen castle. This is situated on the Swansea to Llandeilo Road, around 5 miles from Pentregwenlais, and Sian and Rhys both loved going there. The vie from the keep was delightful, there were refreshments available and a cafe and Bookshop at the visitor centre.

It was as if there was a spring in my step all the way back to London on the return journey that Sunday.

It is ironic that my last such trip, made after my stay on the ICSL course had finally concluded, would provoke such disparate emotions from my family.

The one thing that strikes me as being missing from this memoir and its Dramatis personae (or, it's 'List of Characters') is a long term , or 'life's partner'..

I guess I have only twice, ever, been considered to be a 'catch' for someone. One ended in divorce after over 11 years of marriage but produced 2 lovely children along the way. The other relationship ended only with the premature death of Harriet from Cancer.

Maybe I am being greedy. But it would be nice to get another partner. Someone to while away the hours with, share likes, co-exist with dislikes, but nevertheless, brighten the place and my life up a bit.

LIFE AFTER MARRIAGE: MIDDLE AGED PURSUITS

In December of 2000, I turned 40 years of age.

I was lodging with a young lady in a house in Walthamstow, London E17.

We had originally met through our mutual involvement with The London Forest Choir (LFC).

I had first joined that chorus of keen, very talented choral singers way back in 1983, at the same time that I was establishing myself as a pharmacist.

They rehearsed weekly, on Monday evenings after normal working hours and attracted a wide variety of people, from all walks of life, to their ranks.

The sang a range of music; from the well established choral masterpieces, such as Mendelssohn'e 'Elijah' to modern, atonal works such as Francis Poulenc's 'Gloria'. They also went on singing tours to the near European continent. Many choristers were reasonably wealthy in that they had well paid jobs. Therefore, LFC were able to go on tours to places like Northern France, North Germany and even Padova, in Italy.

Therefore, by the time a reached 40 years of age and my 5th decade, I had a very fulfilling and satisfying way of life.

At the first LFC rehearsal following my birthday, I noticed a new person had decided to join LFC. She looked intriguing. Not exactly pretty. But she had a confident deportment and a definite 'Je ne sais qua' about her. Nowadays, the word 'Riz' has entered the mainstream vocabulary after being included in the Oxford English Dictionery's 'Words of the Year' list a couple of years ago and I thought she had 'Riz', - Charisma in plenty.

I made a point of speaking to her at tea-break. Her name was Harriet, and she had been widowed. She had joined LFC due to the advice of friends simply in order to 'get (herself) out of the house, and thereby to seek to rebuild her life after the death, at a young age, of her husband.

I was immediately smitten!

Over the 2 or 3 subsequent LFC rehearsals, we would speak during breaks and then, go for a drink with other chorus members in a local pub afterwards.

Soon, we were an item!

I discovered that she had 2 children; 1 of each sex, and that became an easy talking point with Rhys and Sian's exploits and achievements being a comparison to Harriet's son and daughter. In fact, my Sian and Harriet's daughter were the same age, both having been born in 1988.

As time went on, Harriet and me became; not so much an 'Item' but partners. We began to do everything together. We had a lot of fun. We went on foreign singing tours, concerts, meals and drinks out, and I spent almost as much time at Harriet's little house as I did, alone m at my own! I also began to think of re-marrying after my divorce from Maria had become absolute in 2007. But Harriet did not want to re-marry. At the last count, I had asked her to marry me on a total of 4 separate occasions during the 17 years that we were together. But each time, she refused!

I understand. The circumstances whereby Harriet had lost her own husband had not been of her making, and therefore, it never seemed appropriate to raise the topic in her presence and certainly, never to ask questions about the circumstances of his death over a Christmastime while their children were still very young.

Harriet and I would just have 'fun' We were both musical, both liked choral singing and during one rehearsal, s choir friend of mine mentioned to me that another group were short of men for an upcoming performance. Would I like to help them out? Ever keen to please, I said 'Yes'. Thus began my association with the works if Gilbert and Sullivan.

The first time I attended the 'Lantern Light Opera' s rehearsal for a rehearsal night was at a village hall in Chigwell, Essex in 2007. I didn't"t really know what expect but, kidding myself that I was capable of keeping an open mind, I presumed it would be rather like an ordinary LFC choir practice.

I couldn't have been more wrong.

Instead of well-ordered rows of chairs arranged for seating the 4 different voice parts; Soprano, Alto, Tenor and Bass, any chairs (and there weren't too many of those!), any chais that were set out were arranged around the perimeter instead. The evening's rehearsal participants began to drift in, including the man who had suggested the group to me as being of potential interest.. There then appeared the group's piano accompanist and the session's conductor, or music director. I spoke to one or two of the participants and was made to feel very welcome.

But even before the group began to 'warm-up' its voices, I could hear a marked difference in the type of repertoire we would be singing. The music seemed to be far more jaunty and one or two participants were singing different pieces to everyone else. Choral singers, whatever they're particular voice parts might be, are fundamentally, performing the same musical piece or work as all the other chorus members. Here, there were shorter, more informal sounding solo singer sections. Some were male soloists, others female. I learned that the performance was to actually be over 4 nights and a run of the Gilbert & Sullivan operetta 'Patience'. Someone lent me a copy of the work's vocal score. Much of the time during that rehearsal, I was silent. This, to me, seemed rather frustrating. But there were 1 or 2 sections where by Bass colleagues and I were required on our own. I diligently attended the few remaining rehearsals and discovered that, in fact, I had only joined the group halfway through the show's overall rehearsal schedule.

The next big surprise when I was informed that I would need to be fitted out for the costumes. Very quickly, I would learn that I was to be a 'Heavy Dragoon' guard during the 4 night run. By the time show week arrived, I was confident that I would be able to do the production justice both as one of the singers, but also as an actor in character throughout. It was clear to me that this latest venture was to be in a different league from what I had done before.

I invited Harriet to come and see a performance. She duly came, but seemed a bit non-plussed when I informed her I would have to go and get changed separately. She looked even more agog when she next saw me; kitted out in my 'Heavy Dragoon' outfit alongside the rest of the male chorus.

Of course, I would not be in a position to judge what Harriet had actually thought about the production itself. But when I asked her, she said she had enjoyed it.

The next project that Lantern Light Opera mounted was earmarked for the following spring. It would be of 'The Zoo' by Bolton Rowe and Arthur Sullivan together with a medley of songs from some of Gilbert & Sullivan's better known operas.

Thus time Harriet took the opportunity to sing herself. She had been born into a musical and show biz family. Her father was a musically trained professional circus clown who appeared at the famous Blackpool circus and her mother had been a 'Tiller Girl' in London's West End before starting a family.

We performed a duet. It was 'Koko' and 'Katisha's duet from The Mikado 'There is beauty in the bellow of the blast'. Harriet was very good and understood the musical requirements perfectly.

I then suggested to her that we should join a specialist Gilbert & Sullivan performance group or an operatic group to join alongside our LFC exploits. She readily agreed. The 'Chapel End Savoy Players' (CESP) seemed perfect as it was based in Walthamstow and so, not so very far away from where I lived and within 2 or 3 miles of Harriet's house.

Over the next decade and more, I managed to appear in each of the annual productions CESP performed until, sadly, the group folded in 2019. I was even cast in several principal roles, my favourite being as Sgt. Meryll in 'The Yeomen of the Guard' in 2014.

ACKNOWLEDGMENTS

1. The counter staff at the Port Talbot Public Library service; who have accurately, courteously and efficiently assisted with my frequent, technical queries.

2. My surviving son, Rhys John, and his family for their unswerving support over the years.

3. The players and staff at Aberavon R.F.C who have provided focus and entertainment over the many hundreds of times I have been present to watch them play. Since the first time I was able to experience the vibrancy of match days at the Talbot Athletic Ground from the very first occasion, a 6 - 5 victory against local rivals, Neath as far back, possibly, as the 1965-66 season when I was taken to watch the match from the terraces, through the lean results during the rest of the 1960s, to the successful days of the mid, and late, 1970s, through the frustrations of defeat in each of the 4 occasions they managed to reach the Welsh challenge cup final and even the 1976-77 season when they managed to beat local rivals, Neath, on no less than 4 occasions, at home and away during their club's centenary season.

LEISURE ACTIVITIES AND MY MUSICAL TASTES AND ADVENTURES IN PARTICULAR

I have always preferred 'Classical' music to any other genre.

I believe I can trace that preference to the early times of my exposure to music and musicians and concerts.

My father oversaw my earliest musical memories. He used to take a few piano pupils for lessons in a room at our house in Margam. There seemed to be a steady progression of boys and girls coming to our house during the 1960s and early '70s. Most would not attend for more than one or two lessons. A few stayed a little longer before giving up. But, he had one 'star' Pupil. A girl you have already met. The Type 1 Diabetic girl. Her name was Alison Lehman and she lived only a few doors from us in Margam. She passed her Grade 8 Royal College of Music (RCM) practical and theory exam but, sadly, she died, while still a young woman several years ago.

The piano became, in due course, the musical instrument I had most success with. It is probably right to claim that that was due to the affinity I garnered while pottering about with it, at home and at secondary school.

My regret is that I didn't pursue any practical musicianship through school and thereafter.

My life's record of 1 'Distinction' grading at the Royal Schools of Music (RSM) piano exam at Grade 1 that I achieved as an 11 year old in 1972, and Grade 'A' at my GSE (now known as GCSE)

As I move into the mid point of my seventh decade, my life's record of one 'A' grade at 'O' level (now called, GCSE) and 1 'Distinction' assessment at the Royal School of Music Grade 1 exam when I was 11 years old, in 1972, is nothing to 'write home about' After all, I have not sought any public recognition for the standard of my playing; I have not been paid,(or asked) to perform in public other than on a couple of 'come and Play' evenings during my Chapel End Savoy Players time in Walthamstow between 2007 and 2019.

POSTSCRIPT.

As I write this memoir, I recall the fondest memories of all who are named herein. I can honestly record that, among the many people I have mentioned by name, I cannot think of a single individual, group, or institution that I would now class as an enemy. To those loved ones who are no longer here, my late Daughter; Sian Elizabeth Amanda John (4 April 1988 - 5 August 2016). Thanks for being the beautiful, mischievous, lively and straightforward girl that you were over your 28 years of eventful, but always loving, life.

To both my parents for raising me through all the difficult times from my birth, my childhood, my teenage years, and, after I left home to pursue whatever I wanted to do. And, of course, their willingness to fund my endeavours. At all times, both evidenced a strong moral undercurrent to their lives. I hope that I have inherited that undercurrent.

Equally, I hope that Rhys, and his young family will live, and enjoy, long lives well after I have gone!

www.ingramcontent.com/pod-product-compliance
Lightning Source LLC
Chambersburg PA
CBHW081000120626
46546CB00010B/2979